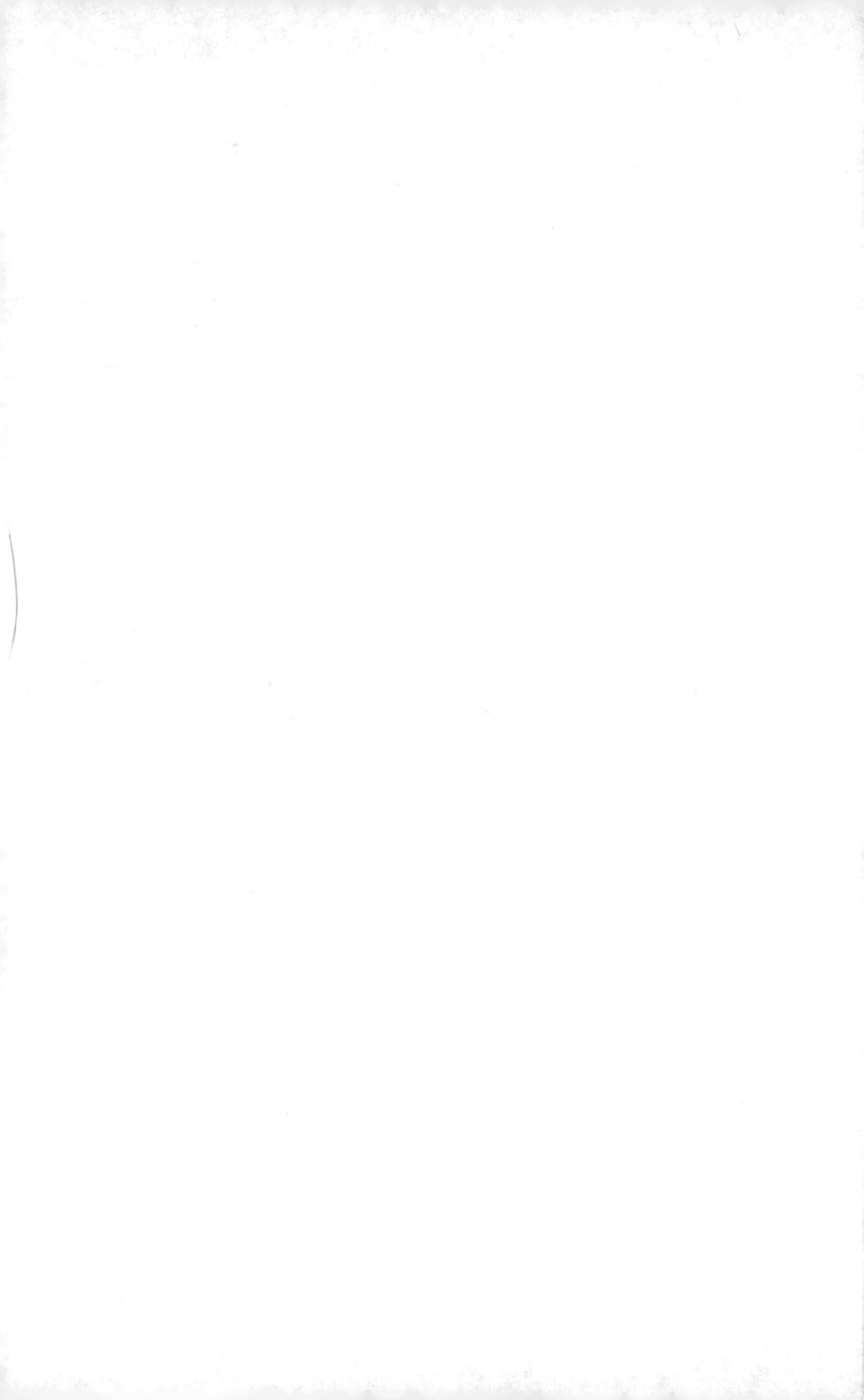

Python 3 Data Visualization Using Google Gemini

Companion files for this title are available by writing to the publisher at info@merclearning.com.

Python 3 Data Visualization Using Google Gemini

Oswald Campesato

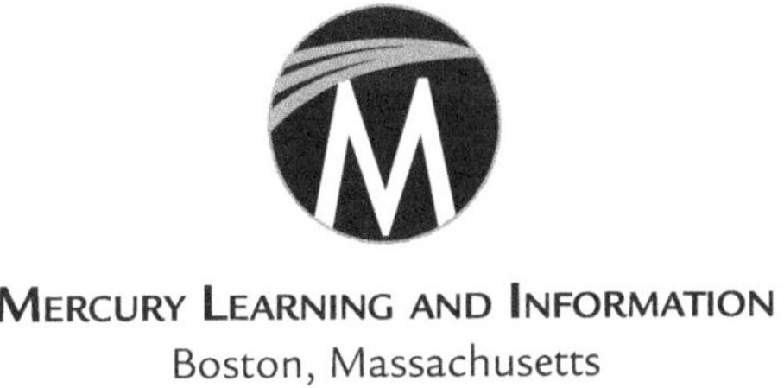

Mercury Learning and Information
Boston, Massachusetts

Publisher: David Pallai
Mercury Learning and Information
121 High Street, 3rd Floor
Boston, MA 02110
info@merclearning.com
www.merclearning.com
800-232-0223

O. Campesato. *Python 3 Data Visualization Using Google Gemini.*
ISBN: 978-1-50152-280-2

Library of Congress Control Number: 2024932122
242526321 This book is printed on acid-free paper in the United States of America.

Our titles are available for adoption, license, or bulk purchase by institutions, corporations, etc. For additional information, please contact the Customer Service Dept. at 800-232-0223(toll free).

All of our titles are available in digital format at academiccourseware.com and other digital vendors. *Companion files (figures and code listings) for this title are available by contacting info@merclearning.com.* The sole obligation of Mercury Learning and Information to the purchaser is to replace the files, based on defective materials or faulty workmanship, but not based on the operation or functionality of the product.

I'd like to dedicate this book to my parents – may this bring joy and happiness into their lives.

CONTENTS

PREFACE

WHAT IS THE PRIMARY VALUE PROPOSITION FOR THIS BOOK?

This book offers a comprehensive guide to leveraging Python-based data visualization techniques with the innovative capabilities of Google Gemini. Tailored for individuals proficient in Python seeking to enhance their visualization skills, this book explores essential libraries like Pandas, Matplotlib, and Seaborn, along with insights into the innovative Gemini platform. With a focus on practicality and efficiency, it delivers a rapid yet thorough exploration of data visualization methodologies, supported by insightful Bard-generated code samples.

CONTENT HIGHLIGHTS

The first chapter contains a quick tour of basic `Python` 3, followed by a chapter that introduces you to `NumPy`. The third and fourth chapters introduce you to data visualization with `Matplotlib` and how to create graphics effects with `Seaborn`. The fifth chapter introduces you to Google Gemini, which also includes a discussion of GPT-4. The sixth and concluding chapter contains Gemini-generated Python code samples for performing various programming tasks.

WHY ARE THE CODE SAMPLES PRIMARILY IN PYTHON?

Most of the code samples are short (usually less than one page and sometimes less than half a page), and if necessary, you can easily and quickly copy/paste the code into a new Jupyter notebook. For the Python code samples that reference a `CSV` file, you do not need any additional code in the corresponding Jupyter notebook to access the `CSV` file.

Moreover, the code samples execute quickly, so you won't need to avail yourself of the free GPU that is provided in Google Colaboratory.

If you do decide to use Google Colaboratory, you can easily copy/paste the `Python` code into a notebook, and also use the upload feature to upload existing Jupyter notebooks. Keep in mind the following point: if the `Python` code references a `csv` file, make sure that you include the appropriate code snippet (details are available online) to access the `csv` file in the corresponding Jupyter notebook in Google Colaboratory.

WHY DOES THIS BOOK INCLUDE SKLEARN MATERIAL?

First, keep in mind that the Sklearn material in this book is minimalistic because this book is not about machine learning. Second, the Sklearn material is located in chapter 4 where you will learn about some of the Sklearn built-in datasets. If you decide to research machine learning, you will have already been introduced to some aspects of Sklearn.

WHAT DO I NEED TO KNOW FOR THIS BOOK?

Current knowledge of `Python 3.x` is the most helpful skill. Knowledge of other programming languages (such as Java) can also be helpful because of the exposure to programming concepts and constructs. The less technical knowledge that you have, the more diligence will be required in order to understand the assorted topics that are covered.

As for the non-technical skills, it is important to have a strong desire to learn about data visualization, along with the motivation and discipline to read and understand code samples.

DOES THIS BOOK CONTAIN PRODUCTION-LEVEL CODE SAMPLES?

The primary purpose of the code samples in this book is to show you `Python`-based libraries for data visualization. Clarity has higher priority than writing more compact code that is more difficult to understand (and more prone to bugs). If you decide to use any of the code in this book on a production website, you ought to subject that code to the same rigorous analysis as the other parts of your code base.

HOW DO I SET UP A COMMAND SHELL?

If you are a Mac user, there are three ways to do so. The first method is to use `Finder` to navigate to `Applications > Utilities` and then double click on the `Utilities` application. Next, if you already have a command shell available, you can launch a new command shell by typing the following command:

```
open /Applications/Utilities/Terminal.app
```

A second method for Mac users is to open a new command shell on a MacBook from a command shell that is already visible simply by clicking `command+n` in that command shell, and your Mac will launch another command shell.

If you are a PC user, you can install Cygwin (open source *https://cygwin.com/*) that simulates bash commands or use another toolkit such as MKS (a commercial product). Please read the online documentation that describes the download and installation process. Note that custom aliases are not automatically set if they are defined in a file other than the main start-up file (such as .bash_login).

COMPANION FILES

All the code samples and figures in this book may be obtained by writing to the publisher at *info@merclearning.com*.

O. Campesato
February 2024

CHAPTER 1

INTRODUCTION TO PYTHON

This chapter contains an introduction to Python, with information about useful tools for installing modules, basic constructs, and how to work with some data types.

The first part of this chapter covers how to install Python, some environment variables, and how to use the interpreter. You will see code samples and also how to save code in text files that you can launch from the command line. The second part of this chapter shows you how to work with simple data types, such as numbers, fractions, and strings. The final part of this chapter discusses exceptions and how to use them in scripts.

NOTE *The Python files in this book are for Python 3.x.*

TOOLS FOR PYTHON

The Anaconda Python distribution available for Windows, Linux, and Mac is downloadable at *http://continuum.io/downloads*.

Anaconda is well-suited for modules such as `numpy` and `scipy`, and if you are a Windows user, Anaconda appears to be a better alternative.

easy_install and pip

Both `easy_install` and `pip` are easy to use when you need to install Python modules. Whenever you need to install a module (and there are many in this book), use either `easy_install` or `pip` with the following syntax:

```
easy_install <module-name>
pip install <module-name>
```

NOTE *Python-based modules are easier to install, whereas modules with code written in C are usually faster but more difficult in terms of installation.*

virtualenv

The `virtualenv` tool enables you to create isolated Python environments, and its home page is at *http://www.virtualenv.org/en/latest/virtualenv.html.*

`virtualenv` addresses the problem of preserving the correct dependencies and versions (and indirectly, permissions) for different applications. If you are a Python novice, you might not need `virtualenv` right now, but keep this tool in mind.

IPython

Another very good tool is IPython (which won a Jolt award), and its home page is at *http://ipython.org/install.html.* Two very nice features of IPython are tab expansion and "?" (textual assistance). An example of tab expansion is shown here:

```
$ python
Python 3.9.1 (v3.9.1:1e5d33e9b9, Dec 7 2020, 12:44:01)
[Clang 12.0.0 (clang-1200.0.32.27)] on darwin
Type "help", "copyright", "credits" or "license" for more
information.

IPython 0.13.2 -- An enhanced Interactive Python.
?         -> Introduction and overview of IPython's
             features.
%quickref -> Quick reference.
help      -> Python's own help system.
object?   -> Details about 'object', use 'object??' for
extra details.

In [1]: di
%dirs   dict    dir     divmod
```

In the preceding session, if you type the characters `di`, IPython responds with the following line that contains all the functions that start with the letters `di`:

```
%dirs   dict    dir     divmod
```

If you enter a question mark ("?"), IPython provides textual assistance, the first part of which is here:

```
IPython -- An enhanced Interactive Python
=========================================

IPython offers a combination of convenient shell features,
special commands and a history mechanism for both input
(command history) and output (results caching, similar
to Mathematica). It is intended to be a fully compatible
replacement for the standard Python interpreter, while
offering vastly improved functionality and flexibility.
```

The next section shows you how to check whether Python is installed on your machine, and also where you can download Python.

PYTHON INSTALLATION

Before you download anything, check if you have Python already installed on your machine (which is likely if you have a MacBook or a Linux machine) by typing the following command in a command shell:

```
python -V
```

The output for the MacBook used in this book is here:

```
Python 3.9.1
```

NOTE *Install Python 3.9 (or as close as possible to this version) on your machine so that you will have the same version of Python that was used to test the Python files in this book.*

If you need to install Python on your machine, navigate to the Python home page and select the downloads link or navigate directly to this website:

http://www.python.org/download/

In addition, PythonWin is available for Windows, and its home page is here:

http://www.cgl.ucsf.edu/Outreach/pc204/pythonwin.html

Use any text editor that can create, edit, and save Python scripts, and save them as plain text files (do not use Microsoft Word). After you have Python installed and configured on your machine, you are ready to work with the Python scripts in this book.

SETTING THE PATH ENVIRONMENT VARIABLE (WINDOWS ONLY)

The `PATH` environment variable specifies a list of directories that are searched whenever you specify an executable program from the command line. The following URL has a useful guide to setting up your environment so that the Python executable is always available in every command shell:

http://www.blog.pythonlibrary.org/2011/11/24/python-101-setting-up-python-on-windows/

LAUNCHING PYTHON ON YOUR MACHINE

There are three different ways to launch Python:

- Use the Python Interactive Interpreter.
- Launch Python scripts from the command line.
- Use an IDE.

The next section shows you how to launch the Python interpreter from the command line, and later in this chapter you will learn how to launch scripts from the command line and also about IDEs.

NOTE *The emphasis in this book is to launch Python scripts from the command line or to enter code in the Python interpreter.*

The Python Interactive Interpreter

Launch the interactive interpreter from the command line by opening a command shell and typing the following command:

```
python
```

You will see the following prompt (or something similar):

```
Python 3.9.1 (v3.9.1:1e5d33e9b9, Dec  7 2020, 12:44:01)
[Clang 12.0.0 (clang-1200.0.32.27)] on darwin
Type "help", "copyright", "credits" or "license" for more information.
>>>
```

Now type the expression `2 + 7` at the prompt:

```
>>> 2 + 7
```

Python displays the following result:

```
9
>>>
```

enter `quit()` to exit the Python shell.

You can launch any Python script from the command line by preceding it with the word "python." For example, if you have a script `myscript.py` that contains commands, launch the script as follows:

```
python myscript.py
```

As a simple illustration, suppose that the script `myscript.py` contains the following code:

```
print('Hello World from Python')
print('2 + 7 = ', 2+7)
```

When you launch the preceding script, you will see the following output:

```
Hello World from Python
2 + 7 =  9
```

PYTHON IDENTIFIERS

An *identifier* is the name of a variable, function, class, module, or other Python object, and a valid identifier conforms to the following rules:

- starts with a letter A to Z or a to z or an underscore (_)
- zero or more letters, underscores, and digits (0 to 9)

NOTE *Python identifiers cannot contain characters such as @, $, and %.*

Python is a case-sensitive language, so `Abc` and `abc` are different identifiers in Python. In addition, Python has the following naming conventions:

- Class names start with an uppercase letter and all other identifiers with a lowercase letter
- An initial underscore is used for private identifiers.
- Two initial underscores are used for strongly private identifiers.

A Python identifier with two initial underscores and two trailing underscore characters indicates a language-defined special name.

LINES, INDENTATION, AND MULTI-LINE COMMENTS

Unlike other programming languages (such as Java or Objective-C), Python uses indentation instead of curly braces for code blocks. Indentation must be consistent in a code block, as shown here:

```
if True:
    print("ABC")
    print("DEF")
else:
    print("ABC")
    print("DEF")
```

Multi-line statements in Python can terminate with a new line or the backslash ("\") character, as shown here:

```
total = x1 + \
        x2 + \
        x3
```

Obviously, you can place `x1`, `x2`, and `x3` on the same line, so there is no reason to use three separate lines; however, this functionality is available in case you need to add a set of variables that do not fit on a single line.

You can specify multiple statements in one line by using a semicolon (";") to separate each statement, as shown here:

```
a=10; b=5; print(a); print(a+b)
```

The output of the preceding code snippet is here:

```
10
15
```

NOTE *The use of semi-colons and the continuation character are discouraged in Python.*

QUOTATIONS AND COMMENTS IN PYTHON

Python allows single ('), double ("), and triple (''' or """) quotation marks for string literals, provided that they match at the beginning and the end of the string. You can use triple quotation marks for strings that span multiple lines. The following examples are legal Python strings:

```
word = 'word'
line = "This is a sentence."
para = """This is a paragraph. This paragraph contains
more than one sentence."""
```

A string literal that begins with the letter "r" (for "raw") treats everything as a literal character and "escapes" the meaning of meta characters, as shown here:

```
a1 = r'\n'
a2 = r'\r'
a3 = r'\t'
print('a1:',a1,'a2:',a2,'a3:',a3)
```

The output of the preceding code block is here:

```
a1: \n a2: \r a3: \t
```

You can embed a single quotation mark in a pair of double quotation marks (and vice versa) to display a single quotation mark or double quotation marks. Another way to accomplish the same result is to precede single or double quotation marks with a backslash ("\") character. The following code block illustrates these techniques:

```
b1 = "'"
b2 = '"'
b3 = '\''
b4 = "\""
print('b1:',b1,'b2:',b2)
print('b3:',b3,'b4:',b4)
```

The output of the preceding code block is here:

```
b1: ' b2: "
b3: ' b4: "
```

A hash sign (#) that is not inside a string literal is the character that indicates the beginning of a comment. Moreover, all characters after the # and up to the physical line end are part of the comment (and ignored by the Python interpreter). Consider the following code block:

```
#!/usr/bin/python
# First comment
print("Hello, Python!")  # second comment
```

This will produce following result:

```
Hello, Python!
```

A comment may be on the same line after a statement or expression:

```
name = "Tom Jones" # This is also comment
```

You can comment multiple lines as follows:

```
# This is comment one
# This is comment two
# This is comment three
```

A blank line in Python is a line containing only whitespace, a comment, or both.

SAVING YOUR CODE IN A MODULE

Earlier you saw how to launch the Python interpreter from the command line and then enter commands. However, everything you type in the Python interpreter is only valid for the current session: if you exit the interpreter and then launch the interpreter again, your previous definitions are no longer valid. Fortunately, Python enables you to store code in a text file, as discussed in the next section.

A *module* in Python is a text file that contains Python statements. In the previous section, you saw how the interpreter enables you to test code snippets whose definitions are valid for the current session. If you want to retain the code snippets and other definitions, place them in a text file so that you can execute that code outside of the interpreter.

The outermost statements in a Python program are executed from top to bottom when the module is imported for the first time, which will then set up its variables and functions.

A Python module can be run directly from the command line, as shown here:

```
python first.py
```

As an illustration, place the following two statements in a text file called `first.py`:

```
x = 3
print(x)
```

Now type the following command:

```
python first.py
```

The output from the preceding command is `3`, which is the same as executing the preceding code from the interpreter.

When a module is run directly, the special variable `__name__` is set to `__main__`. You will often see the following type of code in a module:

```
if __name__ == '__main__':
    # do something here
    print('Running directly')
```

The preceding code snippet enables Python to determine if a module was launched from the command line or imported into another module.

SOME STANDARD MODULES IN PYTHON

The Python Standard Library provides many modules that can simplify your own scripts. A list of the Standard Library modules is at *http://www.python.org/doc/*.

Some of the most important modules include `cgi`, `math`, `os`, `pickle`, `random`, `re`, `socket`, `sys`, `time`, and `urllib`.

The code samples in this book use the modules `math`, `os`, `random`, `re`, `socket`, `sys`, `time`, and `urllib`. You need to import these modules to use them in your code. For example, the following code block shows you how to import 4 standard Python modules:

```
import datetime
import re
import sys
import time
```

The code samples in this book import one or more of the preceding modules, as well as other Python modules.

THE help() AND dir() FUNCTIONS

An Internet search for Python-related topics usually returns a number of links with useful information. Alternatively, you can check the official Python documentation site: *docs.python.org*.

In addition, Python provides the `help()` and `dir()` functions that are accessible from the interpreter. The `help()` function displays documentation strings, whereas the `dir()` function displays defined symbols.

For example, if you type `help(sys)` you will see documentation for the `sys` module, whereas `dir(sys)` displays a list of the defined symbols.

Type the following command in the interpreter to display the string-related methods in Python:

```
>>> dir(str)
```

The preceding command generates the following output:

```
['__add__', '__class__', '__contains__', '__delattr__',
'__doc__', '__eq__', '__format__', '__ge__', '__
getattribute__', '__getitem__', '__getnewargs__', '__
```

```
getslice__', '__gt__', '__hash__', '__init__', '__le__',
'__len__', '__lt__', '__mod__', '__mul__', '__ne__',
'__new__', '__reduce__', '__reduce_ex__', '__repr__',
'__rmod__', '__rmul__', '__setattr__', '__sizeof__',
'__str__', '__subclasshook__', '_formatter_field_name_
split', '_formatter_parser', 'capitalize', 'center',
'count', 'decode', 'encode', 'endswith', 'expandtabs',
'find', 'format', 'index', 'isalnum', 'isalpha', 'isdigit',
'islower', 'isspace', 'istitle', 'isupper', 'join',
'ljust', 'lower', 'lstrip', 'partition', 'replace',
'rfind', 'rindex', 'rjust', 'rpartition', 'rsplit',
'rstrip', 'split', 'splitlines', 'startswith', 'strip',
'swapcase', 'title', 'translate', 'upper', 'zfill']
```

The preceding list gives you a consolidated "dump" of built-in functions (including some that are discussed later in this chapter). Although the `max()` function obviously returns the maximum value of its arguments, the purpose of other functions such as `filter()` or `map()` is not immediately apparent (unless you have used them in other programming languages). The preceding list provides a starting point for finding out more about various Python built-in functions that are not discussed in this chapter.

Note that while `dir()` does not list the names of built-in functions and variables, you can obtain this information from the standard module `__builtin__` that is automatically imported under the name `__builtins__`:

```
>>> dir(__builtins__)
```

The following command shows you how to get more information about a function:

```
help(str.lower)
```

The output from the preceding command is here:

```
Help on method_descriptor:

lower(...)
    S.lower() -> string

    Return a copy of the string S converted to lowercase.
(END)
```

Check the online documentation and also experiment with `help()` and `dir()` when you need additional information about a particular function or module.

COMPILE TIME AND RUNTIME CODE CHECKING

Python performs some compile-time checking, but most checks (including type, name, and so forth) are *deferred* until code execution. Consequently, if your Python code references a user-defined function that does not exist, the code will compile successfully. In fact, the code will fail with an exception *only* when the code execution path references the non-existent function.

As a simple example, consider the following function `myFunc` that references the non-existent function called `DoesNotExist`:

```
def myFunc(x):
    if x == 3:
        print(DoesNotExist(x))
    else:
        print('x: ',x)
```

When `myFunc()` is invoked with the value 3, the "if" conditional is true, at which point the `print()` statement will fail because `DoesNotExist()` does not exist.

In Chapter 2, you will learn how to define and invoke user-defined functions, along with an explanation of the difference between local versus global variables in Python.

Now that you understand some basic concepts (such as how to use the Python interpreter) and how to launch your custom modules, the next section discusses primitive data types.

SIMPLE DATA TYPES

Python supports primitive data types, such as numbers (integers, floating point numbers, and exponential numbers), strings, and dates. Python also supports more complex data types, such as lists (or arrays), tuples, and dictionaries, all of which are discussed in Chapter 3. The next several sections discuss some of the Python primitive data types, along with code snippets that show you how to perform various operations on those data types.

WORKING WITH NUMBERS

Python provides arithmetic operations for manipulating numbers in a straightforward manner that is similar to other programming languages. The following examples involve arithmetic operations on integers:

```
>>> 2+2
4
>>> 4/3
1
>>> 3*8
24
```

The following example assigns numbers to two variables and computes their product:

```
>>> x = 4
>>> y = 7
>>> x * y
28
```

The following examples demonstrate arithmetic operations involving integers:

```
>>> 2+2
4
>>> 4/3
1
>>> 3*8
24
```

Notice that division ("/") of two integers is actually truncation in which only the integer result is retained. The following example converts a floating point number into exponential form:

```
>>> fnum = 0.00012345689000007
>>> "%.14e"%fnum
'1.23456890000070e-04'
```

You can use the `int()` function and the `float()` function to convert strings to numbers:

```
word1 = "123"
word2 = "456.78"
var1 = int(word1)
var2 = float(word2)
print("var1: ",var1," var2: ",var2)
```

The output from the preceding code block is here:

```
var1:  123  var2:  456.78
```

Alternatively, you can use the `eval()` function:

```
word1 = "123"
word2 = "456.78"
var1 = eval(word1)
var2 = eval(word2)
print("var1: ",var1," var2: ",var2)
```

If you attempt to convert a string that is not a valid integer or a floating point number, Python raises an exception, so it is advisable to place your code in a `try/except` block.

Working with Other Bases

Numbers in Python are in base 10 (the default), but you can easily convert numbers to other bases. For example, the following code block initializes the variable x with the value `1234`, and then displays that number in base `2`, `8`, and `16`:

```
>>> x = 1234
>>> bin(x) '0b10011010010'
>>> oct(x) '0o2322'
>>> hex(x) '0x4d2' >>>
```

Use the `format()` function if you want to suppress the `0b`, `0o`, or `0x` prefixes, as shown here:

```
>>> format(x, 'b') '10011010010'
>>> format(x, 'o') '2322'
>>> format(x, 'x') '4d2'
```

Negative integers are displayed with a negative sign:

```
>>> x = -1234
>>> format(x, 'b') '-10011010010'
>>> format(x, 'x') '-4d2'
```

The chr() Function

The `chr()` function takes a positive integer as a parameter and converts it to its corresponding alphabetic value (if one exists). The letters A through Z have decimal representation of `65` through `91` (which corresponds to hexadecimal `41` through `5b`), and the lowercase letters `a` through `z` have decimal representation `97` through `122` (hexadecimal `61` through `7b`).

Here is an example of using the `chr()` function to print uppercase `A`:

```
>>> x=chr(65)
>>> x
'A'
```

The following code block prints the ASCII values for a range of integers:

```
result = ""
for x in range(65,90):
  print(x, chr(x))
  result = result+chr(x)+' '
print("result: ",result)
```

NOTE *Python 2 uses ASCII strings whereas Python 3 uses Unicode.*

You can represent a range of characters with the following line:

```
for x in range(65,90):
```

However, the following equivalent code snippet is more intuitive:

```
for x in range(ord('A'), ord('Z')):
```

If you want to display the result for lowercase letters, change the preceding range from `(65,91)` to either of the following statements:

```
for x in range(65,90):
for x in range(ord('a'), ord('z')):
```

The round() Function

The `round()` function enables you to round decimal values to the nearest precision:

```
>>> round(1.23, 1)
1.2
>>> round(-3.42,1)
-3.4
```

Formatting Numbers

Python allows you to specify the number of decimal places of precision to use when printing decimal numbers, as shown here:

```
>>> x = 1.23456
>>> format(x, '0.2f')
'1.23'
>>> format(x, '0.3f')
'1.235'
>>> 'value is {:0.3f}'.format(x) 'value is 1.235'
>>> from decimal import Decimal
>>> a = Decimal('4.2')
>>> b = Decimal('2.1')
>>> a + b
Decimal('6.3')
>>> print(a + b)
6.3
>>> (a + b) == Decimal('6.3')
True
>>> x = 1234.56789
>>> # Two decimal places of accuracy
>>> format(x, '0.2f')
'1234.57'
>>> # Right justified in 10 chars, one-digit accuracy
>>> format(x, '>10.1f')
' 1234.6'
>>> # Left justified
>>> format(x, '<10.1f') '1234.6 '
>>> # Centered
>>> format(x, '^10.1f') ' 1234.6 '
>>> # Inclusion of thousands separator
>>> format(x, ',')
'1,234.56789'
>>> format(x, '0,.1f')
'1,234.6'
```

WORKING WITH FRACTIONS

Python supports the `Fraction()` function (defined in the `fractions` module), which accepts two integers that represent the numerator and the denominator (which must be non-zero) of a fraction. Several examples of defining and manipulating fractions are shown here:

```
>>> from fractions import Fraction
>>> a = Fraction(5, 4)
>>> b = Fraction(7, 16)
>>> print(a + b)
27/16
>>> print(a * b) 35/64
>>> # Getting numerator/denominator
>>> c = a * b
```

```
>>> c.numerator
35
>>> c.denominator 64
>>> # Converting to a float >>> float(c)
0.546875
>>> # Limiting the denominator of a value
>>> print(c.limit_denominator(8))
4
>>> # Converting a float to a fraction >>> x = 3.75
>>> y = Fraction(*x.as_integer_ratio())
>>> y
Fraction(15, 4)
```

Before delving into code samples that work with strings, the next section briefly discusses Unicode and UTF-8, both of which are character encodings.

UNICODE AND UTF-8

A Unicode string consists of a sequence of numbers that are between `0` and `0x10ffff`, where each number represents a group of bytes. An *encoding* is the manner in which a Unicode string is translated into a sequence of bytes. Among the various encodings, UTF-8 ("Unicode Transformation Format") is perhaps the most common, and it is also the default encoding for many systems. The digit 8 in UTF-8 indicates that the encoding uses 8-bit numbers, whereas UTF-16 uses 16-bit numbers (but this encoding is less common).

The ASCII character set is a subset of UTF-8, so a valid ASCII string can be read as a UTF-8 string without any re-encoding required. In addition, a Unicode string can be converted into a UTF-8 string.

WORKING WITH UNICODE

Python supports Unicode, which means that you can render characters in different languages. Unicode data can be stored and manipulated in the same way as strings. Create a Unicode string by prepending the letter `u`, as shown here:

```
>>> u'Hello from Python!'
u'Hello from Python!'
```

Special characters can be included in a string by specifying their Unicode value. For example, the following Unicode string embeds a space (which has the Unicode value 0x0020) in a string:

```
>>> u'Hello\u0020from Python!'
u'Hello from Python!'
```

Listing 1.1 displays the content of `unicode1.py` that illustrates how to display a string of characters in Japanese and another string of characters in Chinese (Mandarin).

LISTING 1.1: unicode1.py

```
chinese1 = u'\u5c07\u63a2\u8a0e HTML5 \u53ca\u5176\u4ed6'
hiragana = u'D3 \u306F \u304B\u3063\u3053\u3043\u3043 \
u3067\u3059!'

print('Chinese:',chinese1)
print('Hiragana:',hiragana)
```

The output of Listing 1.2 is here:

```
Chinese: 將探討 HTML5 及其他
Hiragana: D3 は かっこぃぃ です!
```

The next portion of this chapter shows you how to "slice and dice" text strings with built-in Python functions.

WORKING WITH STRINGS

You can concatenate two strings using the "+" operator. The following example prints a string and then concatenates two single-letter strings:

```
>>> 'abc'
'abc'
>>> 'a' + 'b'
'ab'
```

You can use "+" or "*" to concatenate identical strings, as shown here:

```
>>> 'a' + 'a' + 'a'
'aaa'
>>> 'a' * 3
'aaa'
```

You can assign strings to variables and print them using the `print()` command:

```
>>> print('abc')
abc
>>> x = 'abc'
>>> print(x)
abc
>>> y = 'def'
>>> print(x + y)
abcdef
```

You can "unpack" the letters of a string and assign them to variables, as shown here:

```
>>> str = "World"
>>> x1,x2,x3,x4,x5 = str
>>> x1
```

```
'W'
>>> x2
'o'
>>> x3
'r'
>>> x4
'l'
>>> x5
'd'
```

The preceding code snippets show you how easy it is to extract the letters in a text string, and in Chapter 3 you will learn how to "unpack" other data structures.

You can extract substrings of a string as shown in the following examples:

```
>>> x = "abcdef"
>>> x[0]
'a'
>>> x[-1]
'f'
>>> x[1:3]
'bc'
>>> x[0:2] + x[5:]
'abf'
```

However, you will cause an error if you attempt to "subtract" two strings:

```
>>> 'a' - 'b'
Traceback (most recent call last):
  File "<stdin>", line 1, in <module>
TypeError: unsupported operand type(s) for -: 'str' and
'str'
```

The `try/except` construct enables you to handle the preceding type of exception gracefully.

Comparing Strings

You can use the methods `lower()` and `upper()` to convert a string to lowercase and uppercase, respectively, as shown here:

```
>>> 'Python'.lower()
'python'
>>> 'Python'.upper()
'PYTHON'
>>>
```

The methods `lower()` and `upper()` are useful for performing a case-insensitive comparison of two ASCII strings. Listing 1.2 displays the content of `compare.py` that uses the `lower()` function to compare two ASCII strings.

LISTING 1.2: compare.py

```
x = 'Abc'
y = 'abc'

if(x == y):
  print('x and y: identical')
elif (x.lower() == y.lower()):
  print('x and y: case insensitive match')
else:
  print('x and y: different')
```

Since `x` contains mixed case letters and `y` contains lowercase letters, Listing 1.2 displays the following output:

```
x and y: different
```

Formatting Strings

Python provides the functions `string.lstring()`, `string.rstring()`, and `string.center()` for positioning a text string so that it is left-justified, right-justified, and centered, respectively. As you saw in a previous section, Python also provides the `format()` method for advanced interpolation features.

Now enter the following commands in the interpreter:

```
import string

str1 = 'this is a string'
print(string.ljust(str1, 10))
print(string.rjust(str1, 40))
print(string.center(str1,40))
```

The output is shown here:

```
this is a string
                        this is a string
            this is a string
```

The next portion of this chapter shows you how to "slice and dice" text strings with built-in functions.

SLICING AND SPLICING STRINGS

Python enables you to extract substrings of a string (called "slicing") using array notation. Slice notation is `start:stop:step`, where the start, stop, and step values are integers that specify the start value, end value, and the increment value, respectively. The interesting part about slicing in Python is that you can use the value `-1`, which operates from the right-side instead of the left-side of a string.

Some examples of slicing a string are here:

```
text1 = "this is a string"
print('First 7 characters:',text1[0:7])
print('Characters 2-4:',text1[2:4])
print('Right-most character:',text1[-1])
print('Right-most 2 characters:',text1[-3:-1])
```

The output from the preceding code block is here:

```
First 7 characters: this is
Characters 2-4: is
Right-most character: g
Right-most 2 characters: in
```

Later in this chapter, you will see how to insert a string in the middle of another string.

Testing for Digits and Alphabetic Characters

Python enables you to examine each character in a string and then test whether that character is a bona fide digit or an alphabetic character. This section provides a precursor to regular expressions that are discussed in Chapter 4.

Listing 1.3 displays the content of `char_types.py` that illustrates how to determine if a string contains digits or characters. In case you are unfamiliar with the conditional "if" statement in Listing 1.3, more detailed information is available in Chapter 2.

LISTING 1.3: char_types.py

```
str1 = "4"
str2 = "4234"
str3 = "b"
str4 = "abc"
str5 = "a1b2c3"

if(str1.isdigit()):
  print("this is a digit:",str1)

if(str2.isdigit()):
  print("this is a digit:",str2)

if(str3.isalpha()):
  print("this is alphabetic:",str3)

if(str4.isalpha()):
  print("this is alphabetic:",str4)

if(not str5.isalpha()):
  print("this is not pure alphabetic:",str5)

print("capitalized first letter:",str5.title())
```

Listing 1.3 initializes some variables, followed by 2 conditional tests that check whether `str1` and `str2` are digits using the `isdigit()` function. The next portion of Listing 1.3 checks if `str3`, `str4`, and `str5` are alphabetic strings using the `isalpha()` function. The output of Listing 1.3 is here:

```
this is a digit: 4
this is a digit: 4234
this is alphabetic: b
this is alphabetic: abc
this is not pure alphabetic: a1b2c3
capitalized first letter: A1B2C3
```

SEARCH AND REPLACE A STRING IN OTHER STRINGS

Python provides methods for searching and replacing a string in a second text string. Listing 1.4 displays the content of `find_pos1.py` that shows you how to use the find function to search for the occurrence of one string in another string.

LISTING 1.4: find_pos1.py

```
item1 = 'abc'
item2 = 'Abc'
text = 'This is a text string with abc'

pos1 = text.find(item1)
pos2 = text.find(item2)

print('pos1=',pos1)
print('pos2=',pos2)
```

Listing 1.4 initializes the variables `item1`, `item2`, and `text`, and then searches for the index of the contents of `item1` and `item2` in the string text. The `find()` function returns the column number where the first successful match occurs; otherwise, the `find()` function returns a `-1` if a match is unsuccessful.

The output from launching Listing 1.4 is here:

```
pos1= 27
pos2= -1
```

In addition to the `find()` method, you can use the `in` operator when you want to test for the presence of an element, as shown here:

```
>>> lst = [1,2,3]
>>> 1 in lst
True
```

Listing 1.5 displays the content of `replace1.py` that shows you how to replace one string with another string.

LISTING 1.5: replace1.py

```
text = 'This is a text string with abc'
print('text:',text)
text = text.replace('is a', 'was a')
print('text:',text)
```

Listing 1.5 starts by initializing the variable text and then printing its contents. The next portion of Listing 1.5 replaces the occurrence of "is a" with "was a" in the string text, and then prints the modified string. The output from launching Listing 1.5 is here:

```
text: This is a text string with abc
text: This was a text string with abc
```

REMOVE LEADING AND TRAILING CHARACTERS

Python provides the functions `strip()`, `lstrip()`, and `rstrip()` to remove characters in a text string. Listing 1.6 displays the content of `remove1.py` that shows you how to search for a string.

LISTING 1.6: remove1.py

```
text = '   leading and trailing white space     '
print('text1:','x',text,'y')

text = text.lstrip()
print('text2:','x',text,'y')

text = text.rstrip()
print('text3:','x',text,'y')
```

Listing 1.6 starts by concatenating the letter `x` and the contents of the variable `text`, and then printing the result. The second part of Listing 1.6 removes the leading white spaces in the string `text` and then appends the result to the letter `x`. The third part of Listing 1.6 removes the trailing white spaces in the string `text` (note that the leading white spaces have already been removed) and then appends the result to the letter `x`.

The output from launching Listing 1.6 is here:

```
text1: x    leading and trailing white space     y
text2: x leading and trailing white space     y
text3: x leading and trailing white space y
```

If you want to remove extra white spaces inside a text string, use the `replace()` function, as discussed in the previous section. The following example illustrates how this can be accomplished, which also contains the `re` module as a "preview" for what you will learn in Chapter 4:

```
import re
text = 'a    b'
```

```
a = text.replace(' ', '')
b = re.sub('\s+', ' ', text)

print(a)
print(b)
```

The result is here:

```
ab
a b
```

Chapter 2 shows you how to use the `join()` function to remove extra white spaces in a text string.

PRINTING TEXT WITHOUT NEWLINE CHARACTERS

If you need to suppress white space and a newline between objects output with multiple `print()` statements, you can use concatenation or the `write()` function.

The first technique is to concatenate the string representations of each object using the `str()` function prior to printing the result. For example, run the following statement in `Python`:

```
x = str(9)+str(0xff)+str(-3.1)
print('x: ',x)
```

The output is shown here:

```
x:  9255-3.1
```

The preceding line contains the concatenation of the numbers `9` and `255` (which is the decimal value of the hexadecimal number `0xff`) and `-3.1`.

Incidentally, you can use the `str()` function with modules and user-defined classes. An example involving the Python built-in module `sys` is here:

```
>>> import sys
>>> print(str(sys))
<module 'sys' (built-in)>
```

The following code snippet illustrates how to use the `write()` function to display a string:

```
import sys
write = sys.stdout.write
write('123')
write('123456789')
```

The output is here:

```
123123456789
```

TEXT ALIGNMENT

Python provides the methods `ljust()`, `rjust()`, and `center()` for aligning text. The `ljust()` and `rjust()` functions left justify and right justify a text string, respectively, whereas the `center()` function will center a string. An example is shown in the following code block:

```
text = 'Hello World'
text.ljust(20)
'Hello World '
>>> text.rjust(20)
' Hello World'
>>> text.center(20)
' Hello World '
```

You can use the `format()` function to align text. Use the <, >, or ^ characters, along with a desired width, in order to right justify, left justify, and center the text, respectively. The following examples illustrate how you can specify text justification:

```
>>> format(text, '>20')
'         Hello World'
>>>
>>> format(text, '<20')
'Hello World         '
>>>
>>> format(text, '^20')
'    Hello World     '
>>>
```

WORKING WITH DATES

Python provides a rich set of date-related functions. Listing 1.7 displays the content of the script `date_time2.py` that displays various date-related values, such as the current date and time; the day of the week, month, and year; and the time in seconds since the epoch.

LISTING 1.7: date_time2.py

```
import time
import datetime

print("Time in seconds since the epoch: %s" %time.time())
print("Current date and time: " , datetime.datetime.now())
print("Or like this: " ,datetime.datetime.now().
strftime("%y-%m-%d-%H-%M"))

print("Current year: ", datetime.date.today().
strftime("%Y"))
print("Month of year: ", datetime.date.today().
strftime("%B"))
```

```
print("Week number of the year: ", datetime.date.today().
strftime("%W"))
print("Weekday of the week: ", datetime.date.today().
strftime("%w"))
print("Day of year: ", datetime.date.today().
strftime("%j"))
print("Day of the month : ", datetime.date.today().
strftime("%d"))
print("Day of week: ", datetime.date.today().
strftime("%A"))
```

Listing 1.8 displays the output generated by running the code in Listing 1.7.

LISTING 1.8 datetime2.out

```
Time in seconds since the epoch: 1375144195.66
Current date and time:  2013-07-29 17:29:55.664164
Or like this:  13-07-29-17-29
Current year:  2013
Month of year:  July
Week number of the year:  30
Weekday of the week:  1
Day of year:  210
Day of the month :  29
Day of week:  Monday
```

Python allows you to perform arithmetic calculates with date-related values, as shown in the following code block:

```
>>> from datetime import timedelta
>>> a = timedelta(days=2, hours=6)
>>> b = timedelta(hours=4.5)
>>> c = a + b
>>> c.days
2
>>> c.seconds
37800
>>> c.seconds / 3600
10.5
>>> c.total_seconds() / 3600
58.5
```

Converting Strings to Dates

Listing 1.9 displays the content of `string2date.py` that illustrates how to convert a string to a date, and also how to calculate the difference between two dates.

LISTING 1.9: string2date.py

```
from datetime import datetime

text = '2024-08-13'
y = datetime.strptime(text, '%Y-%m-%d')
```

```
z = datetime.now()
diff = z - y
print('Date difference:',diff)
```

The output from Listing 1.9 is shown here:

```
Date difference: -210 days, 18:58:40.197130
```

EXCEPTION HANDLING IN PYTHON

Unlike JavaScript, you cannot add a number and a string in Python. However, you can detect an illegal operation using the `try/except` construct in Python, which is similar to the `try/catch` construct in languages such as JavaScript and Java.

An example of a `try/except` block is here:

```
try:
  x = 4
  y = 'abc'
  z = x + y
except:
  print('cannot add incompatible types:', x, y)
```

When you run the preceding code, the `print()` statement in the `except` code block is executed because the variables `x` and `y` have incompatible types.

Earlier in the chapter, you also saw that subtracting two strings throws an exception:

```
>>> 'a' - 'b'
Traceback (most recent call last):
  File "<stdin>", line 1, in <module>
TypeError: unsupported operand type(s) for -: 'str' and
'str'
```

A simple way to handle this situation is to use a `try/except` block:

```
>>> try:
...   print('a' - 'b')
... except TypeError:
...   print('TypeError exception while trying to subtract
two strings')
... except:
...   print('Exception while trying to subtract two
strings')
...
```

The output from the preceding code block is here:

```
TypeError exception while trying to subtract two strings
```

As you can see, the preceding code block specifies the finer-grained exception called `TypeError`, followed by a generic `except` code block to handle all other exceptions that might occur during the execution of your Python code. This style is similar to the exception handling in Java code.

Listing 1.10 displays the content of exception1.py that illustrates how to handle various types of exceptions.

LISTING 1.10: exception1.py

```
import sys

try:
    f = open('myfile.txt')
    s = f.readline()
    i = int(s.strip())
except IOError as err:
    print("I/O error: {0}".format(err))
except ValueError:
    print("Could not convert data to an integer.")
except:
    print("Unexpected error:", sys.exc_info()[0])
    raise
```

Listing 1.10 contains a try block followed by three except statements. If an error occurs in the try block, the first except statement is compared with the type of exception that occurred. If there is a match, then the subsequent print() statement is executed, and the program terminates. If not, a similar test is performed with the second except statement. If neither except statement matches the exception, the third except statement handles the exception, which involves printing a message and then "raising" an exception. Note that you can also specify multiple exception types in a single statement, as shown here:

```
except (NameError, RuntimeError, TypeError):
    print('One of three error types occurred')
```

The preceding code block is more compact, but you do not know which of the three error types occurred. Python allows you to define custom exceptions, but this topic is beyond the scope of this book.

HANDLING USER INPUT

Python enables you to read user input from the command line via the input() function or the raw_input() function. Typically, you assign user input to a variable, which will contain all characters that users enter from the keyboard. User input terminates when users press the <return> key (which is included with the input characters). Listing 1.11 displays the content of user_input1.py that prompts users for their name and then uses interpolation to display a response.

LISTING 1.11: user_input1.py

```
userInput = input("Enter your name: ")
print ("Hello %s, my name is Python" % userInput)
```

The output of Listing 1.11 is here (assume that the user entered the word `Dave`):

```
Hello Dave, my name is Python
```

The `print()` statement in Listing 1.11 uses string interpolation via `%s`, which substitutes the value of the variable after the `%` symbol. This functionality is obviously useful when you want to specify something that is determined at run-time.

User input can cause exceptions (depending on the operations that your code performs), so it is important to include exception-handling code.

Listing 1.12 displays the content of `user_input2.py` that prompts users for a string and attempts to convert the string to a number in a `try/except` block.

LISTING 1.12: user_input2.py

```
userInput = input("Enter something: ")

try:
  x = 0 + eval(userInput)
  print('you entered the number:',userInput)
except:
  print(userInput,'is a string')
```

Listing 1.12 adds the number `0` to the result of converting a user's input to a number. If the conversion was successful, a message with the user's input is displayed. If the conversion failed, the `except` code block consists of a `print()` statement that displays a message.

NOTE *This code sample uses the* `eval()` *function, which should be avoided so that your code does not evaluate arbitrary (and possibly destructive) commands.*

Listing 1.13 displays the content of `user_input3.py` that prompts users for two numbers and attempts to compute their sum in a pair of `try/except` blocks.

LISTING 1.13: user_input3.py

```
sum = 0

msg = 'Enter a number:'
val1 = input(msg)
```

```
try:
  sum = sum + eval(val1)
except:
  print(val1,'is a string')

msg = 'Enter a number:'
val2 = input(msg)

try:
  sum = sum + eval(val2)
except:
  print(val2,'is a string')

print('The sum of',val1,'and',val2,'is',sum)
```

Listing 1.13 contains two `try` blocks, each of which is followed by an `except` statement. The first `try` block attempts to add the first user-supplied number to the variable `sum`, and the second `try` block attempts to add the second user-supplied number to the previously entered number. An error message occurs if either input string is not a valid number; if both are valid numbers, a message is displayed containing the input numbers and their sum. Be sure to read the caveat regarding the `eval()` function that is mentioned earlier in this chapter.

COMMAND-LINE ARGUMENTS

Python provides a `getopt` module to parse command-line options and arguments, and the `sys` module provides access to any command-line arguments via the `sys.argv`. This serves two purposes:

1. `sys.argv` is the list of command-line arguments.
2. `len(sys.argv)` is the number of command-line arguments.

Here, `sys.argv[0]` is the program name, so if the program is called `test.py`, it matches the value of `sys.argv[0]`.

Now you can provide input values for a Python program on the command line instead of providing input values by prompting users for their input.

As an example, consider the script `test.py` shown here:

```
#!/usr/bin/python
import sys
print('Number of arguments:',len(sys.argv),'arguments')
print('Argument List:', str(sys.argv))
```

Now run above script as follows:

```
python test.py arg1 arg2 arg3
```

This will produce following result:

```
Number of arguments: 4 arguments.
Argument List: ['test.py', 'arg1', 'arg2', 'arg3']
```

The ability to specify input values from the command line provides useful functionality. For example, suppose that you have a custom Python class that contains the methods `add` and `subtract` to add and subtract a pair of numbers.

You can use command-line arguments to specify which method to execute on a pair of numbers, as shown here:

```
python MyClass add 3 5
python MyClass subtract 3 5
```

This functionality is very useful because you can programmatically execute different methods in a Python class, which means that you can write unit tests for your code as well. Read Chapter 8 to learn how to create custom classes.

Listing 1.14 displays the content of `hello.py` that shows you how to use `sys.argv` to check the number of command line parameters.

LISTING 1.14: hello.py

```
import sys

def main():
  if len(sys.argv) >= 2:
    name = sys.argv[1]
  else:
    name = 'World'
  print('Hello', name)

# Standard boilerplate to invoke the main() function
if __name__ == '__main__':
  main()
```

Listing 1.14 defines the `main()` function that checks the number of command-line parameters: if this value is at least `2`, then the variable `name` is assigned the value of the second parameter (the first parameter is `hello.py`), otherwise `name` is assigned the value `Hello`. The `print()` statement then prints the value of the variable `name`.

The final portion of Listing 1.14 uses conditional logic to determine whether to execute the `main()` function.

SUMMARY

This chapter showed you how to work with numbers and perform arithmetic operations on numbers, and then you learned how to work with strings and use string operations. You also learned how to use the try/except construct to handle exceptions that might occur in your Python code. The next chapter introduces you to NumPy, along with code samples that illustrate various features of NumPy.

CHAPTER 2

INTRODUCTION TO NUMPY

This chapter provides a quick introduction to the Python NumPy library, which provides very useful functionality, not only for "regular" Python scripts, but also for Python-based scripts with TensorFlow. For instance, you will see NumPy code samples containing loops, arrays, and lists. You will also learn about dot products, the `reshape()` method (very useful!), how to plot with Matplotlib (discussed in more detail in Chapter 4), and examples of linear regression.

The first part of this chapter briefly discusses NumPy and some of its useful features. The second part contains examples of working arrays in NumPy, and contrasts some of the APIs for lists with the same APIs for arrays. In addition, you will see how easy it is to compute the exponent-related values (square, cube, and so forth) of elements in an array.

The second part of the chapter introduces subranges, which are very useful (and frequently used) for extracting portions of datasets in machine learning tasks. In particular, you will see code samples that handle negative (-1) subranges for vectors as well as for arrays, because they are interpreted one way for vectors and a different way for arrays.

The third part of this chapter delves into other NumPy methods, including the `reshape()` method, which is useful (and very common) when working with image files: some TensorFlow APIs require converting a 2D array of `(R,G,B)` values into a corresponding one-dimensional vector.

The fourth part of this chapter delves into linear regression, the mean squared error (MSE), and how to calculate MSE with the NumPy `linspace()` API.

WHAT IS NUMPY?

NumPy is a Python library that provides many convenient methods and improved code performance. NumPy contains a core library for scientific computing in Python, with performant multi-dimensional arrays and vectorized math functions, along with support for linear algebra and random numbers.

NumPy is modeled after MatLab, with support for lists, arrays, and so forth. NumPy is easier to use than MatLab, and it is very common in TensorFlow code as well as Python code.

Useful NumPy Features

The NumPy library contains the `ndarray` object, which encapsulates *multi-dimensional* arrays of homogeneous data types. Many `ndarray` operations are performed in compiled code to improve performance.

There are important differences between NumPy arrays and standard Python sequences. First, NumPy arrays have a fixed size, whereas Python lists can expand dynamically. Second, NumPy arrays are homogeneous, which means that the elements in a NumPy array must have the same data type. Third, NumPy arrays support more efficient execution (and require less code) of various types of operations on large amounts of data.

Now that you have a general idea about NumPy, let's delve into some examples that illustrate how to work with NumPy arrays, which is the topic of the next section.

WHAT ARE NUMPY ARRAYS?

An *array* is a set of consecutive memory locations used to store data. Each item in the array is called an *element*. The number of elements in an array is called the *dimension* of the array. A typical array declaration is shown here:

```
arr1 = np.array([1,2,3,4,5])
```

The preceding code snippet declares `arr1` as an array of five elements, which you can access via `arr1[0]` through `arr1[4]`. Notice that the first element has an index value of 0, the second element has an index value of 1, and so forth. Thus, if you declare an array of 100 elements, then the 100th element has an index value of 99.

NOTE *The first position in a NumPy array has the index "0."*

NumPy treats arrays as vectors. Math operations are performed element-by-element. Remember the following difference: "doubling" an array *multiplies* each element by 2, whereas "doubling" a list *appends* a list to itself.

Listing 2.1 displays the content of `nparray1.py` that illustrates some operations on a NumPy array.

LISTING 2.1: nparray1.py

```
import numpy as np

list1 = [1,2,3,4,5]
print(list1)
```

```
arr1  = np.array([1,2,3,4,5])
print(arr1)

list2 = [(1,2,3),(4,5,6)]
print(list2)

arr2  = np.array([(1,2,3),(4,5,6)])
print(arr2)
```

Listing 2.1 defines the variables `list1` and `list2` (which are Python lists), as well as the variables `arr1` and `arr2` (which are arrays) and prints their values. The output from launching Listing 2.1 is here:

```
[1, 2, 3, 4, 5]
[1 2 3 4 5]
[(1, 2, 3), (4, 5, 6)]
[[1 2 3]
 [4 5 6]]
```

As you can see, Python lists and NumPy arrays are easy to define. Now, we are ready to look at some loop operations for lists and arrays.

WORKING WITH LOOPS

Listing 2.2 displays the content of `loop1.py` that illustrates how to iterate through the elements of a NumPy array and a Python list.

LISTING 2.2: loop1.py

```
import numpy as np

list = [1,2,3]
arr1 = np.array([1,2,3])

for e in list:
  print(e)

for e in arr1:
  print(e)
```

Listing 2.2 initializes the variable `list`, which is a Python list, and also the variable `arr1`, which is a NumPy array. The next portion of Listing 2.2 contains two loops, each of which iterates through the elements in `list` and `arr1`. As you can see, the syntax is identical in both loops. The output from launching Listing 2.2 is here:

```
1
2
3
1
2
3
```

APPENDING ELEMENTS TO ARRAYS (1)

Listing 2.3 displays the content of `append1.py` that illustrates how to append elements to a NumPy array and a Python list.

LISTING 2.3: append1.py

```
import numpy as np

arr1 = np.array([1,2,3])

# these do not work:
#arr1.append(4)
#arr1 = arr1 + [5]

arr1 = np.append(arr1,4)
arr1 = np.append(arr1,[5])

for e in arr1:
  print(e)

arr2 = arr1 + arr1

for e in arr2:
  print(e)
```

Listing 2.3 initializes the variable `arr1`, which is a NumPy array, and also initialize `arr2`, which is another NumPy array. The output from launching Listing 2.3 is here:

```
1
2
3
4
5
2
4
6
8
10
```

APPENDING ELEMENTS TO ARRAYS (2)

Listing 2.4 displays the content of `append2.py` that illustrates how to append elements to a NumPy array and a Python list.

LISTING 2.4: append2.py

```
import numpy as np

arr1 = np.array([1,2,3])
arr1 = np.append(arr1,4)
```

```
for e in arr1:
  print(e)

arr1 = np.array([1,2,3])
arr1 = np.append(arr1,4)

arr2 = arr1 + arr1

for e in arr2:
  print(e)
```

Listing 2.4 initializes the variable `arr1`, which is a NumPy array. Notice that NumPy arrays do not have an "append" method: this method is available through NumPy itself. Another important difference between Python lists and NumPy arrays is that the "+" operator *concatenates* Python lists, whereas this operator *doubles* the elements in a NumPy array. The output from launching Listing 2.4 is here:

```
1
2
3
4
2
4
6
8
```

MULTIPLYING LISTS AND ARRAYS

Listing 2.5 displays the content of `multiply1.py` that illustrates how to multiply elements in a Python list and a NumPy array.

LISTING 2.5: multiply1.py

```
import numpy as np

list1 = [1,2,3]
arr1  = np.array([1,2,3])
print('list:  ',list1)
print('arr1:  ',arr1)
print('2*list:',2*list)
print('2*arr1:',2*arr1)
```

Listing 2.5 contains a Python list called list and a NumPy array called `arr1`. The `print()` statements display the contents of `list1` and `arr1`, as well as the result of doubling `list1` and `arr1`. Recall that "doubling" a Python list is different from doubling a Python array, which you can see in the output from launching Listing 2.5:

```
('list:  ', [1, 2, 3])
('arr1:  ', array([1, 2, 3]))
('2*list:', [1, 2, 3, 1, 2, 3])
('2*arr1:', array([2, 4, 6]))
```

DOUBLING THE ELEMENTS IN A LIST

Listing 2.6 displays the content of `double_list1.py` that illustrates how to double the elements in a Python list.

LISTING 2.6: double_list1.py

```
import numpy as np

list1 = [1,2,3]
list2 = []

for e in list1:
  list2.append(2*e)

print('list1:',list1)
print('list2:',list2)
```

Listing 2.6 contains a Python list called `list1` and an empty Python list called `list2`. The next code snippet iterates through the elements of `list1` and appends them to the variable `list2`. The pair of `print()` statements display the contents of `list1` and `list2` to show you that they are the same. The output from launching Listing 2.6 is here:

```
('list: ', [1, 2, 3])
('list2:', [2, 4, 6])
```

LISTS AND EXPONENTS

Listing 2.7 displays the content of `exponent_list1.py` that illustrates how to compute exponential values of the elements in a Python list.

LISTING 2.7: exponent_list1.py

```
import numpy as np

list1 = [1,2,3]
list2 = []

for e in list1:
  list2.append(e*e) # e*e = squared

print('list1:',list1)
print('list2:',list2)
```

Listing 2.7 contains a Python list called `list1` and an empty Python list called `list2`. The next code snippet iterates through the elements of `list1` and appends the square of each element to the variable `list2`. The pair of `print()` statements displays the contents of `list1` and `list2`. The output from launching Listing 2.7 is here:

```
('list1:', [1, 2, 3])
('list2:', [1, 4, 9])
```

ARRAYS AND EXPONENTS

Listing 2.8 displays the content of `exponent_array1.py` that illustrates how to compute exponents of the elements in a NumPy array.

LISTING 2.8: exponent_array1.py

```
import numpy as np

arr1 = np.array([1,2,3])
arr2 = arr1**2
arr3 = arr1**3

print('arr1:',arr1)
print('arr2:',arr2)
print('arr3:',arr3)
```

Listing 2.8 contains a NumPy array called `arr1` followed by two NumPy arrays called `arr2` and `arr3`. Notice the compact manner in which the NumPy `arr2` is initialized with the square of the elements in in `arr1`, followed by the initialization of the NumPy array `arr3` with the cube of the elements in `arr1`. The three `print()` statements display the contents of `arr1`, `arr2`, and `arr3`. The output from launching Listing 2.8 is here:

```
('arr1:', array([1, 2, 3]))
('arr2:', array([1, 4, 9]))
('arr3:', array([ 1,  8, 27]))
```

MATH OPERATIONS AND ARRAYS

Listing 2.9 displays the content of `mathops_array1.py` that illustrates how to compute exponents of the elements in a NumPy array.

LISTING 2.9: mathops_array1.py

```
import numpy as np

arr1 = np.array([1,2,3])
sqrt = np.sqrt(arr1)
log1 = np.log(arr1)
exp1 = np.exp(arr1)

print('sqrt:',sqrt)
print('log1:',log1)
print('exp1:',exp1)
```

Listing 2.9 contains a NumPy array called `arr1` followed by three NumPy arrays called `sqrt`, `log1`, and `exp1` that are initialized with the square root, log, and exponential value of the elements in `arr1`, respectively. The three print() statements display the contents of sqrt, log1, and exp1. The output from launching Listing 2.9 is here:

```
('sqrt:', array([1.        , 1.41421356, 1.73205081]))
('log1:', array([0.        , 0.69314718, 1.09861229]))
('exp1:', array([2.71828183, 7.3890561,  20.08553692]))
```

WORKING WITH "–1" SUBRANGES WITH VECTORS

Listing 2.10 displays the content of npsubarray2.py that illustrates how to compute exponents of the elements in a NumPy array.

LISTING 2.10: npsubarray2.py

```
import numpy as np

# -1 => "all except the last element in …" (row or col)

arr1  = np.array([1,2,3,4,5])
print('arr1:',arr1)
print('arr1[0:-1]:',arr1[0:-1])
print('arr1[1:-1]:',arr1[1:-1])
print('arr1[::-1]:', arr1[::-1]) # reverse!
```

Listing 2.10 contains a NumPy array called arr1 followed by four print() statements, each of which displays a different subrange of values in arr1. The output from launching Listing 2.10 is here:

```
('arr1:',       array([1, 2, 3, 4, 5]))
('arr1[0:-1]:', array([1, 2, 3, 4]))
('arr1[1:-1]:', array([2, 3, 4]))
('arr1[::-1]:', array([5, 4, 3, 2, 1]))
```

WORKING WITH "–1" SUBRANGES WITH ARRAYS

Listing 2.11 displays the content of np2darray2.py that illustrates how to compute exponents of the elements in a NumPy array.

LISTING 2.11: np2darray2.py

```
import numpy as np

# -1 => "the last element in …" (row or col)

arr1  = np.array([(1,2,3),(4,5,6),(7,8,9),(10,11,12)])
print('arr1:',       arr1)
print('arr1[-1,:]:',  arr1[-1,:])
print('arr1[:,-1]:',  arr1[:,-1])
print('arr1[-1:,-1]:',arr1[-1:,-1])
```

Listing 2.11 contains a NumPy array called `arr1` followed by four `print()` statements, each of which displays a different subrange of values in `arr1`. The output from launching Listing 2.11 is here:

```
(arr1:', array([[1,  2,  3],
                [4,  5,  6],
                [7,  8,  9],
                [10, 11, 12]]))
(arr1[-1,:]]',   array([10, 11, 12]))
(arr1[:,-1]:',   array([3,  6,  9, 12]))
(arr1[-1:,-1]]', array([12]))
```

OTHER USEFUL NUMPY METHODS

In addition to the NumPy methods that you saw in the code samples prior to this section, the following NumPy methods are also useful.

- The method `np.zeros()` initializes an array with 0 values.
- The method `np.ones()` initializes an array with 1 value.
- The method `np.empty()` initializes an array with 0 values.
- The method `np.arange()` provides a range of numbers.
- The method `np.shape()` displays the shape of an object.
- The method `np.reshape()` <= *very useful!*
- The method `np.linspace()` <= *useful in regression*
- The method `np.mean()` computes the mean of a set of numbers.
- The method `np.std()` computes the standard deviation of a set of numbers.

Although the `np.zeros()` and `np.empty()` both initialize a `2D` array with 0, `np.zeros()` requires less execution time. You could also use `np.full(size, 0)`, but this method is the slowest of all three methods.

The `reshape()` method and the `linspace()` method are very useful for changing the dimensions of an array and generating a list of numeric values, respectively. The `reshape()` method often appears in TensorFlow code, and the `linspace()` method is useful for generating a set of numbers in linear regression. More details about the methods `np.reshape()` and `np.linspace()` are provided later in this chapter.

The `mean()` and `std()` methods are useful for calculating the mean and the standard deviation of a set of numbers, respectively. For example, you can use these two methods to resize the values in a Gaussian distribution so that their mean is 0 and the standard deviation is 1. This process is called *standardizing* a Gaussian distribution.

ARRAYS AND VECTOR OPERATIONS

Listing 2.12 displays the content of `array_vector.py` that illustrates how to perform vector operations on the elements in a NumPy array.

LISTING 2.12: array_vector.py

```
import numpy as np

a = np.array([[1,2], [3, 4]])
b = np.array([[5,6], [7,8]])

print('a:        ', a)
print('b:        ', b)
print('a + b:    ', a+b)
print('a - b:    ', a-b)
print('a * b:    ', a*b)
print('a / b:    ', a/b)
print('b / a:    ', b/a)
print('a.dot(b):',a.dot(b))
```

Listing 2.12 contains two NumPy arrays called `a` and `b` followed by eight `print()` statements, each of which displays the result of "applying" a different arithmetic operation to the NumPy arrays `a` and `b`. The output from launching Listing 2.12 is here:

```
('a    :    ', array([[1, 2], [3, 4]]))
('b    :    ', array([[5, 6], [7, 8]]))
('a + b:    ', array([[ 6,  8], [10, 12]]))
('a - b:    ', array([[-4, -4], [-4, -4]]))
('a * b:    ', array([[ 5, 12], [21, 32]]))
('a / b:    ', array([[0, 0], [0, 0]]))
('b / a:    ', array([[5, 3], [2, 2]]))
('a.dot(b):', array([[19, 22], [43, 50]]))
```

NUMPY AND DOT PRODUCTS (1)

Listing 2.13 displays the content of `dotproduct1.py` that illustrates how to perform the dot product on the elements in a NumPy array.

LISTING 2.13: dotproduct1.py

```
import numpy as np

a = np.array([1,2])
b = np.array([2,3])

dot2 = 0
for e,f in zip(a,b):
  dot2 += e*f
```

```
print('a:    ',a)
print('b:    ',b)
print('a*b:  ',a*b)
print('dot1:',a.dot(b))
print('dot2:',dot2)
```

Listing 2.13 contains two NumPy arrays called a and b followed by a simple loop that computes the dot product of a and b. The next section contains five print() statements that display the contents of a and b, as well as their inner product that is calculated in three different ways. The output from launching Listing 2.13 is here:

```
('a:    ', array([1, 2]))
('b:    ', array([2, 3]))
('a*b:  ', array([2, 6]))
('dot1:', 8)
('dot2:', 8)
```

NUMPY AND DOT PRODUCTS (2)

NumPy provides a "dot" method for calculating the inner product of an array of numbers, which uses the same formula used for calculating the inner product of a pair of vectors. Listing 2.14 displays the content of dotproduct2.py that illustrates how to calculate the dot product of two NumPy arrays.

LISTING 2.14: dotproduct2.py

```
import numpy as np

a = np.array([1,2])
b = np.array([2,3])

print('a:           ',a)
print('b:           ',b)
print('a.dot(b):    ',a.dot(b))
print('b.dot(a):    ',b.dot(a))
print('np.dot(a,b):',np.dot(a,b))
print('np.dot(b,a):',np.dot(b,a))
```

Listing 2.14 contains two NumPy arrays called a and b followed by six print() statements that display the contents of a and b, as well as their inner product that is calculated in three different ways. The output from launching Listing 2.14 is here:

```
('a:           ', array([1, 2]))
('b:           ', array([2, 3]))
('a.dot(b):    ', 8)
('b.dot(a):    ', 8)
('np.dot(a,b):', 8)
('np.dot(b,a):', 8)
```

NUMPY AND THE LENGTH OF VECTORS

The *norm* of a vector (or an array of numbers) is the length of a vector, which is the square root of the dot product of a vector with itself. NumPy also provides the "sum" and "square" methods that you can use to calculate the norm of a vector.

Listing 2.15 displays the content of `array_norm.py` that illustrates how to calculate the magnitude ("norm") of a NumPy array of numbers.

LISTING 2.15: array_norm.py

```
import numpy as np

a = np.array([2,3])
asquare = np.square(a)
asqsum  = np.sum(np.square(a))
anorm1  = np.sqrt(np.sum(a*a))
anorm2  = np.sqrt(np.sum(np.square(a)))
anorm3  = np.linalg.norm(a)

print('a:       ',a)
print('asquare:',asquare)
print('asqsum:  ',asqsum)
print('anorm1:  ',anorm1)
print('anorm2:  ',anorm2)
print('anorm3:  ',anorm3)
```

Listing 2.15 contains an initial NumPy array called `a`, followed by the NumPy array `asquare` and the numeric values `asqsum`, `anorm1`, `anorm2`, and `anorm3`. The NumPy array `asquare` contains the square of the elements in the NumPy array `a`, and the numeric value `asqsum` contains the sum of the elements in the NumPy array `asquare`.

Next, the numeric value `anorm1` equals the square root of the sum of the square of the elements in `a`. The numeric value `anorm2` is the same as `anorm1`, computed in a slightly different fashion. Finally, the numeric value `anorm3` is equal to `anorm2`, but as you can see, `anorm3` is calculated via a single NumPy method, whereas `anorm2` requires a succession of NumPy methods.

The last portion of Listing 2.15 consists of six `print()` statements, each of which displays the computed values. The output from launching Listing 2.15 is here:

```
('a:       ', array([2, 3]))
('asquare:', array([4, 9]))
('asqsum:  ', 13)
('anorm1:  ', 3.605551275463989)
('anorm2:  ', 3.605551275463989)
('anorm3:  ', 3.605551275463989)
```

NUMPY AND OTHER OPERATIONS

NumPy provides the "*" operator to multiply the components of two vectors to produce a third vector whose components are the products of the corresponding components of the initial pair of vectors. This operation is called a *Hadamard product*, which is the name of a famous mathematician. If you then add the components of the third vector, the sum is equal to the inner product of the initial pair of vectors.

Listing 2.16 displays the content of `otherops.py` that illustrates how to perform other operations on a NumPy array.

LISTING 2.16: otherops.py

```
import numpy as np

a = np.array([1,2])
b = np.array([3,4])

print('a:             ',a)
print('b:             ',b)
print('a*b:           ',a*b)
print('np.sum(a*b):  ',np.sum(a*b))
print('(a*b.sum()):  ',(a*b).sum())
```

Listing 2.16 contains two NumPy arrays called `a` and `b` followed five `print()` statements that display the contents of `a` and `b`, their Hadamard product, and their inner product that is calculated in two different ways. The output from launching Listing 2.16 is here:

```
('a:             ', array([1, 2]))
('b:             ', array([3, 4]))
('a*b:           ', array([3, 8]))
('np.sum(a*b):  ', 11)
('(a*b.sum()):  ', 11)
```

NUMPY AND THE RESHAPE() METHOD

NumPy arrays support the `reshape()` method, which allows you to restructure the dimensions of an array of numbers. In general, if a NumPy array contains `m` elements, where `m` is a positive integer, then that array can be restructured as an `m1` x `m2` NumPy array, where `m1` and `m2` are positive integers such that `m1*m2 = m`.

Listing 2.17 displays the content of `numpy_reshape.py` that illustrates how to use the `reshape()` method on a NumPy array.

LISTING 2.17: numpy_reshape.py

```
import numpy as np

x = np.array([[2, 3], [4, 5], [6, 7]])
print(x.shape) # (3, 2)

x = x.reshape((2, 3))
print(x.shape) # (2, 3)
print('x1:',x)

x = x.reshape((-1))
print(x.shape) # (6,)
print('x2:',x)

x = x.reshape((6, -1))
print(x.shape) # (6, 1)
print('x3:',x)

x = x.reshape((-1, 6))
print(x.shape) # (1, 6)
print('x4:',x)
```

Listing 2.17 contains a NumPy array called `x` whose dimensions are 3x2, followed by a set of invocations of the `reshape()` method that reshapes the contents of `x`. The first invocation of the `reshape()` method changes the shape of `x` from 3x2 to 2x3. The second invocation changes the shape of `x` from 2x3 to 6x1. The third invocation changes the shape of `x` from 1x6 to 6x1. The final invocation changes the shape of `x` from 6x1 to 1x6 again.

Each invocation of the `reshape()` method is followed by a `print()` statement so that you can see the effect of the invocation. The output from launching Listing 2.17 is here:

```
(3, 2)
(2, 3)
('x1:', array([[2, 3, 4],
       [5, 6, 7]]))
(6,)
('x2:', array([2, 3, 4, 5, 6, 7]))
(6, 1)
('x3:', array([[2],
       [3],
       [4],
       [5],
       [6],
       [7]]))
(1, 6)
```

CALCULATING THE MEAN AND STANDARD DEVIATION

If you need to review these concepts from statistics (and perhaps also the mean, median, and mode as well), please read the appropriate online tutorials.

NumPy provides various built-in methods that perform statistical calculations, such as the following list of methods:

```
np.linspace() <= useful for regression
np.mean()
np.std()
```

The `np.linspace()` method generates a set of equally-spaced numbers between a lower bound and an upper bound. The `np.mean()` and `np.std()` methods calculate the mean and standard deviation, respectively, of a set of numbers. Listing 2.18 displays the content of `sample_mean_std.py` that illustrates how to calculate statistical values from a NumPy array.

LISTING 2.18: sample_mean_std.py

```
import numpy as np

x2 = np.arange(8)
print('mean = ',x2.mean())
print('std  = ',x2.std())

x3 = (x2 - x2.mean())/x2.std()
print('x3 mean = ',x3.mean())
print('x3 std  = ',x3.std())
```

Listing 2.18 contains a NumPy array `x2` that consists of the first eight integers. Next, the `mean()` and `std()` "associated" with `x2` are invoked to calculate the mean and standard deviation, respectively, of the elements of `x2`. The output from launching Listing 2.18 is here:

```
('a:             ', array([1, 2]))
('b:             ', array([3, 4]))
```

CODE SAMPLE WITH MEAN AND STANDARD DEVIATION

The code sample in this section extends the code sample in the previous section with additional statistical values, and the code in Listing 2.19 can be used for any data distribution. Keep in mind that the code sample uses random numbers simply for the purposes of illustration: after you have launched the code sample, replace those numbers with values from a CSV file or some other dataset containing meaningful values.

Moreover, this section does not provide details regarding the meaning of quartiles, but you can learn about quartiles at *https://en.wikipedia.org/wiki/Quartile*.

Listing 2.19 displays the content of `stat_values.py` that illustrates how to display various statistical values from a NumPy array of random numbers.

LISTING 2.19: stat_values.py

```
import numpy as np

from numpy import percentile
from numpy.random import rand

# generate data sample
data = np.random.rand(1000)

# calculate quartiles, min, and max
quartiles = percentile(data, [25, 50, 75])
data_min, data_max = data.min(), data.max()

# print summary information
print('Minimum:  %.3f' % data_min)
print('Q1 value: %.3f' % quartiles[0])
print('Median:   %.3f' % quartiles[1])
print('Mean Val: %.3f' % data.mean())
print('Std Dev:  %.3f' % data.std())
print('Q3 value: %.3f' % quartiles[2])
print('Maximum:  %.3f' % data_max)
```

The data sample (shown in bold) in Listing 2.19 is from a uniform distribution between 0 and 1. The NumPy `percentile()` function calculates a linear interpolation (average) between observations, which is needed to calculate the median on a sample with an even number of values. As you can surmise, the NumPy functions `min()` and `max()` calculate the smallest and largest values in the data sample. The output from launching Listing 2.19 is here:

```
Minimum:  0.000
Q1 value: 0.237
Median:   0.500
Mean Val: 0.495
Std Dev:  0.295
Q3 value: 0.747
Maximum:  0.999
```

Trimmed Mean and Weighted Mean

In addition to the arithmetic mean, there are variants that are known as the trimmed mean (also called the "truncated mean") and the weighted mean.

A *trimmed mean* is a robust estimate (i.e., a metric that is not sensitive to outliers). As a simple example of a trimmed mean, suppose that you have five scores for the evaluation of a product: simply drop the highest and lowest scores and then compute the average of the remaining three scores. If you have multiple sets of five scores, repeat the preceding process and then compute the average of the set of trimmed mean values.

A *weighted mean* is useful when sample data does not represent different groups in a dataset. Assigning a larger weight to groups that are under-represented yields a weighted mean that more accurately represents the various groups in the dataset. However, keep in mind that outliers can affect the mean as well as the weighted mean.

The weighted mean is the same as the expected value. If you are unfamiliar with the notion of an expected value, suppose that the set `P = {p1,p2,...,pn}` is a probability distribution, which means that the numeric values in the set `P` must be non-negative and have a sum equal to 1. In addition, suppose that `V = {v1,v2,...,vn}` is a set of numeric scores that are assigned to `n` features of a product `M`. For example, the values in the set V could be positive integers in some range (e.g., between 1 and 10) that represent "rewards."

Then the *expected value* `E` for that product is computed as follows:

```
E = p1*v1 + p2*v2 + ... + pn*vn
```

The Python code samples in the next several sections contain some rudimentary APIs from Matplotlib. The code samples start with simple examples of line segments, followed by an introduction to Linear Regression.

WORKING WITH LINES IN THE PLANE (OPTIONAL)

This section contains a short review of lines in the Euclidean plane, so you can skip this section if you are comfortable with this topic. A minor point that is often overlooked is that lines in the Euclidean plane have infinite length. If you select two distinct points of a line, then all the points between those two selected points are a *line segment*. A *ray* is a "half infinite" line: when you select one point as an endpoint, then all the points on one side of the line constitute a ray.

For example, the points in the plane whose y-coordinate is 0 form a line along the x-axis, whereas the points between (0,0) and (1,0) on the x-axis form a line segment. In addition, the points on the x-axis that are to the right of (0,0) form a ray, and the points on the x-axis that are to the left of (0,0) also form a ray.

For simplicity and convenience, in this book we will use the terms "line" and "line segment" interchangeably. Now, let's delve into the details of lines in the Euclidean plane. Here is the equation of a (non-vertical) line in the Euclidean plane:

```
y = m*x + b
```

The value of `m` is the slope of the line and the value of `b` is the y-intercept (i.e., the place where the non-vertical line intersects the y-axis). The following form for a line in the plane is a general equation that includes vertical lines:

```
a*x + b*y + c = 0
```

However, we will not be working with vertical lines, so we will continue using the first formula. Figure 2.1 displays three horizontal lines whose equations (from top to bottom) are `y = 3`, `y = 0`, and `y = -3`.

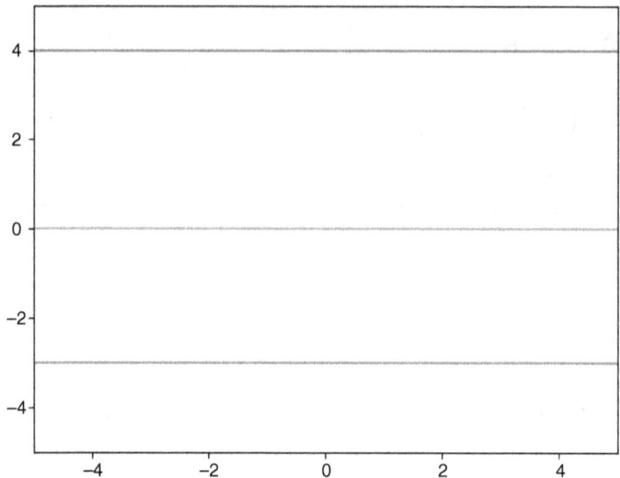

FIGURE 2.1 A graph of three horizontal line segments

Figure 2.2 displays two slanted lines whose equations are y = x and y = -x.

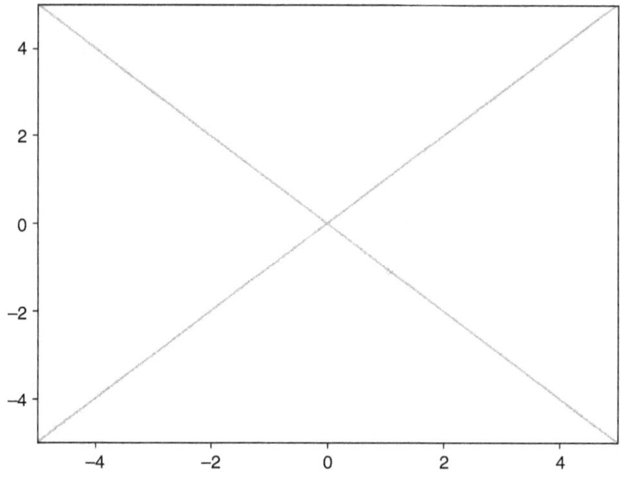

FIGURE 2.2 A graph of two diagonal line segments

Figure 2.3 displays two slanted parallel lines whose equations are `y = 2*x` and `y = 2*x+3`.

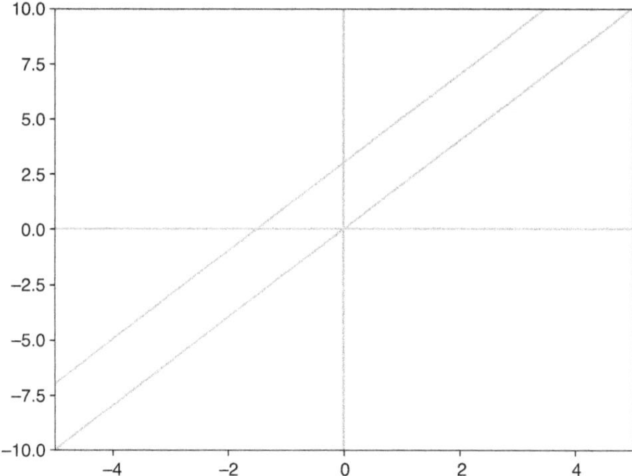

FIGURE 2.3 A graph of two slanted parallel line segments

Figure 2.4 displays a piece-wise linear graph consisting of connected line segments.

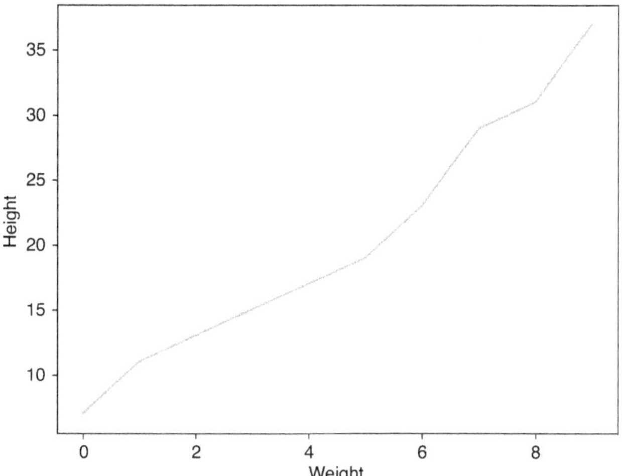

FIGURE 2.4 A piece-wise linear graph of line segments

Now that you have seen some basic examples of lines in the Euclidean plane, let's look at some code samples that use NumPy and Matplotlib to display scatterplots of points in the plane.

PLOTTING RANDOMIZED POINTS WITH NUMPY AND MATPLOTLIB

The previous section contains simple examples of line segments, but the code is deferred until Chapter 3. This section and the next section contain code samples with Matplotlib APIs that are not discussed; however, the code is straightforward, so you can infer its purpose. In addition, you can learn more about Matplotlib in Chapter 7 (which focuses on data visualization) or read a short online tutorial for more details.

Listing 2.20 displays the content of `np_plot.py` that illustrates how to plot multiple points on a line in the plane.

LISTING 2.20: np_plot.py

```
import numpy as np
import matplotlib.pyplot as plt

x = np.random.randn(15,1)
y = 2.5*x + 5 + 0.2*np.random.randn(15,1)

plt.scatter(x,y)
plt.show()
```

Listing 2.20 starts with two `import` statements, followed by the initialization of `x` as a set of random values via the NumPy `randn()` API. Next, `y` is assigned a range of values that consist of two parts: a linear equation with input values from the `x` values, which is combined with a randomization factor. Figure 2.5 displays the output generated by the code in Listing 2.20.

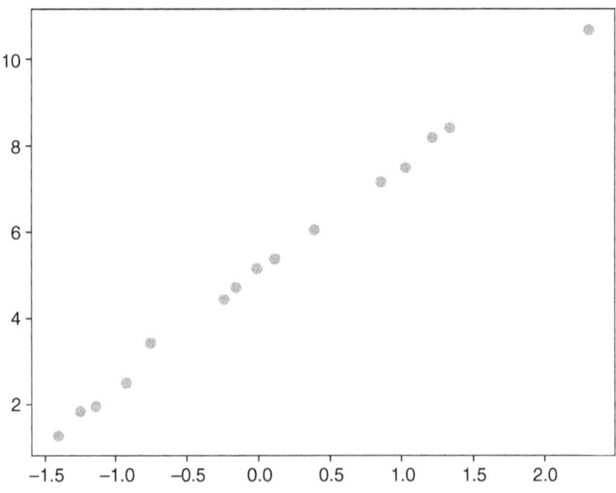

FIGURE 2.5 Datasets with potential linear regression

PLOTTING A QUADRATIC WITH NUMPY AND MATPLOTLIB

Listing 2.21 displays the content of `np_plot_quadratic.py` that illustrates how to plot a quadratic function in the plane.

LISTING 2.21: np_plot_quadratic.py

```
import numpy as np
import matplotlib.pyplot as plt

x = np.linspace(-5,5,num=100)[:,None]
y = -0.5 + 2.2*x +0.3*x**3+ 2*np.random.randn(100,1)

plt.plot(x,y)
plt.show()
```

Listing 2.21 starts with two `import` statements, followed by the initialization of `x` as a range of values via the NumPy `linspace()` API. Next, `y` is assigned a range of values that fit a quadratic equation, which are based on the values for the variable `x`. Figure 2.6 displays the output generated by the code in Listing 2.21.

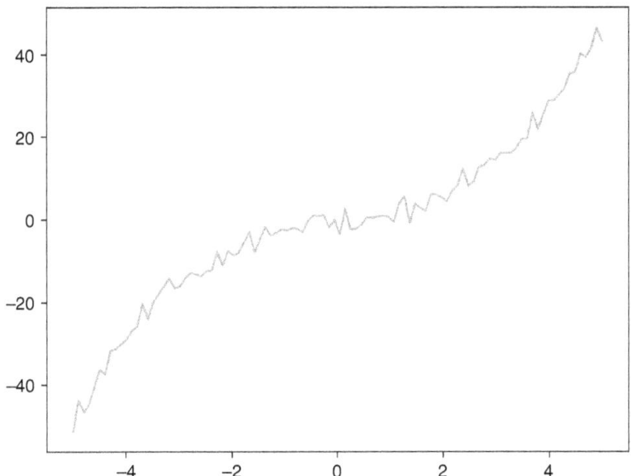

FIGURE 2.6 Datasets with potential linear regression, showing the output generated by the code in Listing 2.21

Now that you have seen an assortment of line graphs and scatterplots, let's delve into linear regression, which is the topic of the next section.

WHAT IS LINEAR REGRESSION?

Linear regression was created in 1805, and it is an important algorithm in statistical analysis and machine learning. Any decent statistical package supports linear regression and invariably supports polynomial regression. Linear regression involves lines, which are polynomials with degree one, whereas polynomial regression involves fitting polynomials of degrees greater than one to a dataset.

In general terms, linear regression finds the equation of the best-fitting hyperplane that approximates a dataset, where the hyperplane has degree one less than the dimensionality of the dataset. In particular, if the dataset is in the Euclidean plane, the hyperplane is simply a line; if the dataset is in 3D, the hyperplane is a "regular" plane.

Linear regression is suitable when the points in a dataset are distributed in such a way that they can reasonably be approximated by a hyperplane. If not, then you can try to fit other types of multi-variable polynomial surfaces to the points in the dataset.

Keep in mind two other details. First, the best-fitting hyperplane does not necessarily intersect all (or even most of) the points in the dataset. In fact, the best-fitting hyperplane might not intersect *any* points in the dataset. The purpose of a best-fitting hyperplane is to *approximate* the points in dataset as closely as possible. Second, linear regression is *not* the same as curve fitting, which attempts to find a polynomial that passes through a set of points.

Some details about curve fitting are as follows. Given `n` points in the plane (no two of which have the same `x` value), there is a polynomial of degree less than or equal to `n-1` that passes through those points. Thus, a line (which has degree 1) will pass through any pair of non-vertical points in the plane. For any triple of points in the plane, there is a quadratic equation or a line that passes through those points.

In some cases, a lower degree polynomial is available. For instance, consider the set of 100 points in which the `x` value equals the `y` value: clearly the line `y = x` (a polynomial of degree 1) passes through all of those points.

However, the extent to which a line "represents" a set of points in the plane depends on how closely those points can be approximated by a line.

What is Multivariate Analysis?

Multivariate analysis generalizes the equation of a line in the Euclidean plane, and it has the following form:

```
y = w1*x1 + w2*x2 + . . . + wn*xn + b
```

The preceding equation contains a linear combination of the variables `x1`, `x2`, . . ., `xn`. In this book we will usually work with datasets that involve lines in the Euclidean plane.

What about Non-Linear Datasets?

Simple linear regression finds the line that best fits a dataset, but what happens if the dataset does not fit a line in the plane? This is an excellent point! In such a scenario, we look for other curves to approximate the dataset, such as quadratic, cubic, or higher-degree polynomials. However, these alternatives involve trade-offs, as we will discuss later.

Another possibility is to use a continuous piece-wise linear function, which is a function that comprises a set of line segments, where adjacent line segments are connected. If one or more pairs of adjacent line segments are not connected, then it is a piece-wise linear function (i.e., the function is discontinuous). In either case, line segments have degree one, which involves lower computational complexity than higher order polynomials.

Thus, given a set of points in the plane, try to find the best-fitting line that fits those points after addressing the following questions:

1. How do we know that a line "fits" the data?
2. What if a different type of curve is a better fit?
3. What does "best fit" mean?

One way to check if a line fits the data well is through a simple visual check: display the data in a graph and if the data conforms to the shape of a line reasonably well, then a line might be a good fit. However, this is a subjective decision, and a sample dataset that does not fit a line is displayed in Figure 2.7.

Figure 2.7 displays a dataset containing four points that do not fit a line.

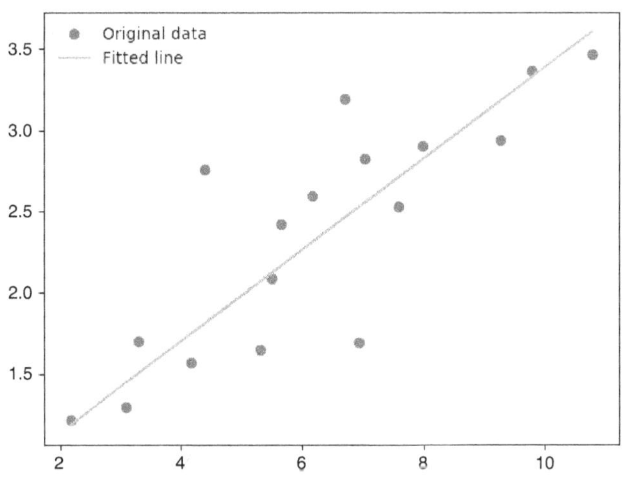

FIGURE 2.7 A non-linear dataset

However, if a line does not appear to be a good fit for the data, then perhaps a quadratic or cubic (or even higher degree) polynomial has the potential of being a better fit. Let's defer the non-linear scenario and make the assumption that a line would be a good fit for the data. There is a well-known technique for finding the best-fitting line for such a dataset: the Mean Squared Error (MSE).

THE MSE (MEAN SQUARED ERROR) FORMULA

Figure 2.8 displays the formula for the MSE. The MSE is the sum of the squares of the difference between an *actual* y value and the *predicted* y value, divided by the number of points. Note that the predicted y value is the y value that each data point would have if that data point were actually on the best-fitting line.

In general, the goal is to minimize the error, which determines the best-fitting line in the case of linear regression. However, you might be satisfied with a "good enough" value when the time and/or cost for any additional reduction in the error is deemed prohibitive, which means that this decision is not a purely programmatic decision.

Figure 2.8 displays the formula for the MSE for calculating the best-fitting line for a set of points in the plane.

$$\text{MSE} = \frac{1}{n}\sum_{i=1}^{n}(Y_i - \hat{Y}_i)^2.$$

FIGURE 2.8 The MSE formula

Other Error Types

Although we only discuss the MSE for linear regression in this book, there are other types of formulas for errors that you can use for linear regression, some of which are listed here:

- MAE
- RMSE
- RMSPROP
- MAE

The MSE is the basis for the preceding error types. For example, the RMSE is the Root Mean Squared Error, which is the square root of the MSE.

The MAE is the Mean Absolute Error, which is *the sum of the absolute value of the differences of the y terms* (not the square of the differences of the y terms).

The RMSProp optimizer utilizes the magnitude of recent gradients to normalize the gradients. Maintain a moving average over the RMS (root mean squared, which is the square root of the MSE) gradients, and then divide that term by the current gradient.

Although it is easier to compute the derivative of the MSE (because it is a differentiable function), it is also true that the MSE is more susceptible to outliers, more so than the MAE. The reason is simple: a squared term can be significantly larger than adding the absolute value of a term. For example, if a difference term is 10, then the squared term 100 is added to the MSE, whereas only 10 is added to the MAE. Similarly, if a difference term is -20, then the squared term 400 is added to the MSE, whereas only 20 (which is the absolute value of -20) is added to the MAE.

Non-Linear Least Squares

When predicting housing prices, where the dataset contains a wide range of values, techniques such as linear regression or random forests can cause the model to "overfit" the samples with the highest values in order to reduce quantities such as the mean absolute error.

In this scenario, you probably want an error metric, such as relative error, that reduces the importance of fitting the samples with the largest values. This technique is called *non-linear least squares*, which may use a log-based transformation of labels and predicted values.

CALCULATING THE MSE MANUALLY

Let's look at two simple graphs, each of which contains a line that approximates a set of points in a scatterplot. Notice that the line segment is the same for both sets of points, but the datasets are slightly different. We will manually calculate the MSE for both datasets and determine which value of the MSE is smaller.

Figure 2.9 displays a set of points and a line that is a potential candidate for best-fitting line for the data.

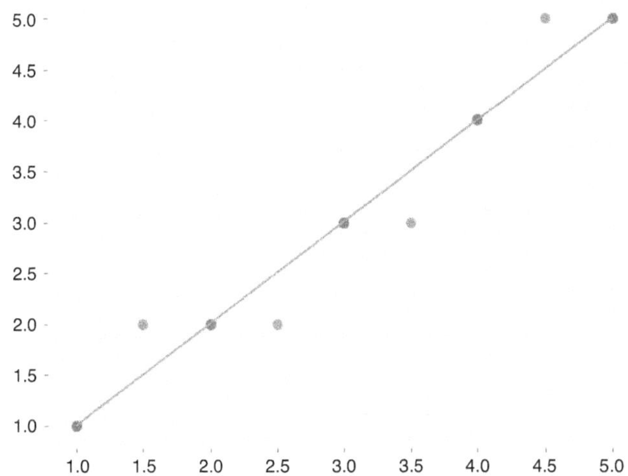

FIGURE 2.9 A line graph that approximates the points of a scatterplot

The MSE for the line in Figure 2.9 is computed as follows:

```
MSE = 1*1 + (-1)*(-1) + (-1)*(-1) + 1*1 = 4
```

Now look at Figure 2.10, which also displays a set of points and a line that is a potential candidate for the best-fitting line of the data.

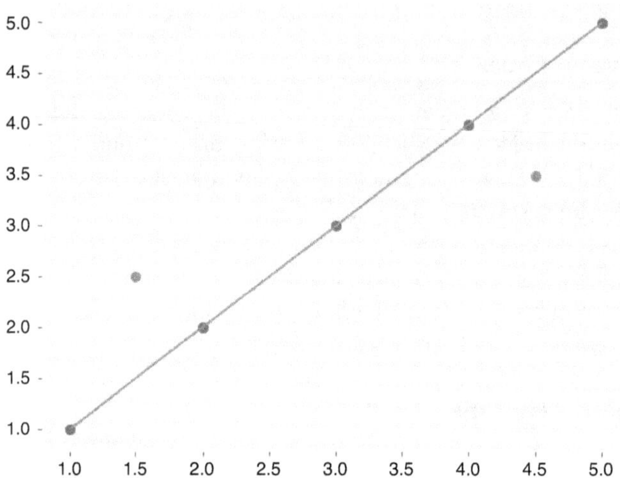

FIGURE 2.10 A line graph that approximates the points of a scatterplot

The `MSE` for the line in Figure 2.10 is computed as follows:

```
MSE = (-2)*(-2) + 2*2 = 8
```

Thus, the line in Figure 2.10 has a smaller `MSE` than the line in Figure 2.9, which might have surprised you (or did you guess correctly?)

In these two figures we calculated the MSE easily and quickly, but in general, it is significantly more difficult. For instance, if we plot 10 points in the Euclidean plane that do not closely fit a line, with individual terms that involve non-integer values, we would probably need a calculator. A better solution involves NumPy functions, as discussed in the next section.

FIND THE BEST-FITTING LINE IN NUMPY

Earlier in this chapter, you saw examples of lines in the plane, including horizontal, slanted, and parallel lines. Most of those lines have a positive slope and a non-zero value for their y-intercept. Although there are scatterplots of data points in the plane where the best-fitting line has a negative slope, the examples in this book involve scatterplots whose best-fitting line has a positive slope.

Listing 2.22 displays the content of `find_best_fit.py` that illustrates how to determine the best-fitting line for a set of points in the Euclidean plane. The solution is based on "closed form" formulas, which are available from statistics.

LISTING 2.22: find_best_fit.py

```
import numpy as np

xs = np.array([1,2,3,4,5], dtype=np.float64)
ys = np.array([1,2,3,4,5], dtype=np.float64)

def best_fit_slope(xs,ys):
  m = (((np.mean(xs)*np.mean(ys))-np.mean(xs*ys)) /
       ((np.mean(xs)**2) - np.mean(xs**2)))
  b = np.mean(ys) - m * np.mean(xs)

  return m, b

m,b = best_fit_slope(xs,ys)
print('m:',m,'b:',b)
```

Listing 2.22 starts with two NumPy arrays `xs` and `ys` that are initialized with the first five positive integers. The Python function `best_fit_slope()` calculates the optimal values of `m` (the slope) and `b` (the y-intercept) of a set of numbers. The output from Listing 2.22 is here:

```
m: 1.0 b: 0.0
```

Notice that the NumPy arrays `xs` and `ys` are identical, which means that these points lie on the identity function whose slope is 1. By simple extrapolation, the point (0,0) is also a point on the same line. Hence, the y-intercept of this line must equal 0.

If you are interested, you can search online to find the derivation for the values of `m` and `b`. In this chapter, we will skip the derivation and proceed with examples of calculating the MSE. The first example involves calculating the MSE manually, followed by an example that uses NumPy formulas to perform the calculations.

CALCULATING THE MSE BY SUCCESSIVE APPROXIMATION (1)

This section contains a code sample that uses a simple technique for successively determining better approximations for the slope and y-intercept of the best-fitting line. Recall that an approximation of a derivative is the ratio of "delta y" divided by "delta x." The "delta" values calculate the difference of the y values and the difference of the x values, respectively, of two nearby points `(x1,y1)` and `(x2,y2)` on a function. Hence, the delta-based approximation ratio is `(y2-y1)/(x2-x1)`.

The technique in this section involves a simplified approximation for the "delta" values: we assume that the denominators are equal to 1. As a result, we need only calculate the numerators of the "delta" values: in this code sample, those numerators are the variables `dw` and `db`.

Listing 2.23 displays the content of `plain_linreg1.py` that illustrates how to compute the MSE with simulated data.

LISTING 2.23: plain_linreg1.py

```
import numpy as np
import matplotlib.pyplot as plt

X = [0,0.12,0.25,0.27,0.38,0.42,0.44,0.55,0.92,1.0]
Y = [0,0.15,0.54,0.51,0.34,0.1, 0.19,0.53,1.0,0.58]

losses = []
#Step 1: Parameter initialization
W = 0.45 # the initial slope
b = 0.75 # the initial y-intercept

for i in range(1, 100):
  #Step 2: Calculate Loss
  Y_pred = np.multiply(W, X) + b
  loss_error = 0.5 * (Y_pred - Y)**2
  loss = np.sum(loss_error)/10

  #Step 3: Calculate dw and db
  db = np.sum((Y_pred - Y))
  dw = np.dot((Y_pred - Y), X)
  losses.append(loss)

  #Step 4: Update parameters:
  W = W - 0.01*dw
  b = b - 0.01*db

  if i%10 == 0:
    print("Loss at", i,"iteration = ", loss)

#Step 5: Repeat via a for loop with 1000 iterations

#Plot loss versus # of iterations
print("W = ", W,"& b = ",  b)
plt.plot(losses)
plt.ylabel('loss')
plt.xlabel('iterations (per tens)')
plt.show()
```

Listing 2.23 defines the variables `X` and `Y` that are simple arrays of numbers (this is our dataset). Next, the losses array is initialized as an empty array, and we will append successive loss approximations to this array. The variables `W` and `b` correspond to the slope and y-intercept, and they are initialized with the values 0.45 and 0.75, respectively (feel free to experiment with these values).

The next portion of Listing 2.23 is a for loop that executes 100 times. During each iteration, the variables `Y_pred`, `loss_error`, and `loss` are computed, and they correspond to the predicted value, the error, and the loss, respectively (remember: we are performing linear regression). The value of `loss` (which is the error for the current iteration) is then appended to the `losses` array.

Next, the variables dw and db are calculated: these correspond to the "delta w" and "delta b" that we will use to update the values of W and b, respectively. The code is reproduced here:

```
#Step 4: Update parameters:
W = W - 0.01*dw
b = b - 0.01*db
```

Notice that dw and db are both multiplied by the value 0.01, which is the value of our "learning rate" (experiment with this value as well).

The next code snippet displays the current cost, which is performed every tenth iteration through the loop. When the loop finishes execution, the values of W and b are displayed, and a plot is displayed that shows the cost values on the vertical axis and the loop iterations on the horizontal axis. The output from Listing 2.23 is here:

```
Loss at 10 iteration =  0.04114630674619491
Loss at 20 iteration =  0.026706242729839395
Loss at 30 iteration =  0.024738889446900423
Loss at 40 iteration =  0.023850565034634254
Loss at 50 iteration =  0.0231499048706651
Loss at 60 iteration =  0.02255361434242207
Loss at 70 iteration =  0.0220425055291673
Loss at 80 iteration =  0.021604128492245713
Loss at 90 iteration =  0.021228111750568435
W =  0.47256473531193927 & b =  0.19578262688662174
```

Figure 2.11 displays the plot of cost-versus-iterations for Listing 2.23.

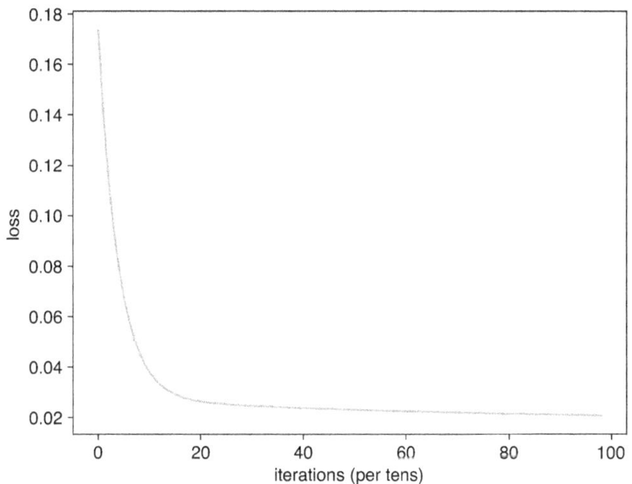

FIGURE 2.11 A plot of cost-versus-iterations

CALCULATING THE MSE BY SUCCESSIVE APPROXIMATION (2)

In the previous section, you saw how to calculate "delta" approximations to determine the equation of a best-fitting line for a set of points in a 2D plane. The example in this section generalizes the code in the previous section by adding an outer loop that represents the number of epochs. The number of epochs specifies the number of times that an inner loop is executed.

Listing 2.24 displays the content of `plain_linreg2.py` that illustrates how to compute the MSE with simulated data.

LISTING 2.24: plain_linreg2.py

```
import numpy as np
import matplotlib.pyplot as plt

# %matplotlib inline
X = [0,0.12,0.25,0.27,0.38,0.42,0.44,0.55,0.92,1.0]
Y = [0,0.15,0.54,0.51, 0.34,0.1,0.19,0.53,1.0,0.58]

#uncomment to see a plot of X versus Y values
#plt.plot(X,Y)
#plt.show()

losses = []
#Step 1: Parameter initialization
W = 0.45
b = 0.75

epochs = 100
lr = 0.001

for j in range(1, epochs):
  for i in range(1, 100):
    #Step 2: Calculate Loss
    Y_pred = np.multiply(W, X) + b
    Loss_error = 0.5 * (Y_pred - Y)**2
    loss = np.sum(Loss_error)/10

    #Step 3: Calculate dW and db
    db = np.sum((Y_pred - Y))
    dw = np.dot((Y_pred - Y), X)
    losses.append(loss)

    #Step 4: Update parameters:
    W = W - lr*dw
    b = b - lr*db

    if i%50 == 0:
      print("Loss at epoch", j,"= ", loss)

#Plot loss versus # of iterations
print("W = ", W,"& b = ",  b)
```

```
plt.plot(losses)
plt.ylabel('loss')
plt.xlabel('iterations (per tens)')
plt.show()
```

Compare the new contents of Listing 2.24 (shown in bold) with the contents of Listing 2.23: the changes are minimal, and the main difference is to execute the inner loop 100 times for each iteration of the outer loop, which also executes 100 times. The output from Listing 2.24 is here:

```
('Loss at epoch', 1, '= ', 0.07161762489862147)
('Loss at epoch', 2, '= ', 0.030073922512586938)
('Loss at epoch', 3, '= ', 0.025415528992988472)
('Loss at epoch', 4, '= ', 0.024227826373677794)
('Loss at epoch', 5, '= ', 0.0234624196707118)
('Loss at epoch', 6, '= ', 0.022827707922883803)
('Loss at epoch', 7, '= ', 0.022284262669854064)
('Loss at epoch', 8, '= ', 0.021817351737166731)
('Loss at epoch', 9, '= ', 0.021416050179776294)
('Loss at epoch', 10, '= ', 0.0210711254093438)
// details omitted for brevity
('Loss at epoch', 90, '= ', 0.018960749188638278)
('Loss at epoch', 91, '= ', 0.01896074755776306)
('Loss at epoch', 92, '= ', 0.018960746155994725)
('Loss at epoch', 93, '= ', 0.018960744951148113)
('Loss at epoch', 94, '= ', 0.018960743915559485)
('Loss at epoch', 95, '= ', 0.018960743025451313)
('Loss at epoch', 96, '= ', 0.018960742260386375)
('Loss at epoch', 97, '= ', 0.018960741602798474)
('Loss at epoch', 98, '= ', 0.018960741037589136)
('Loss at epoch', 99, '= ', 0.018960740551780944)
('W = ', 0.6764145874436108, '& b = ', 0.09976839618922698)
```

Figure 2.12 displays the plot of loss-versus-iterations for Listing 2.24.

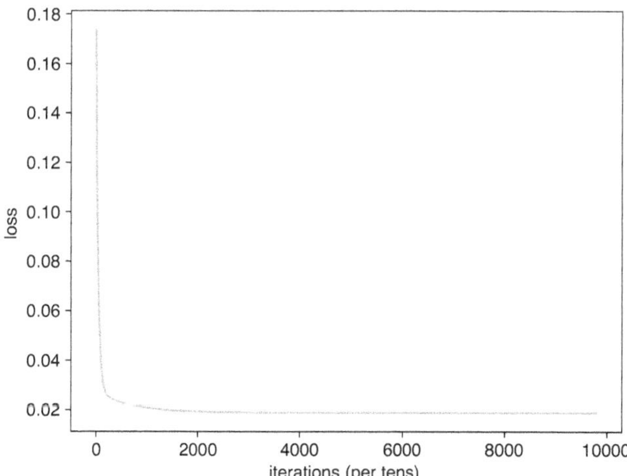

FIGURE 2.12 A plot of loss-versus-iterations

Notice that Figure 2.12 has 10,000 iterations on the horizontal axis, whereas Figure 2.11 has only 100 iterations on the horizontal axis.

GOOGLE COLABORATORY

Depending on the hardware, GPU-based TF 2 code is typically at least 15 times faster than CPU-based TF 2 code. However, the cost of a good GPU can be a significant factor. Although NVIDIA provides GPUs, those consumer-based GPUs are not optimized for multi-GPU support (which *is* supported by TF 2).

Fortunately, Google Colaboratory is an affordable alternative that provides free GPU support, and also runs as a Jupyter notebook environment. In addition, Google Colaboratory executes your code in the cloud and involves zero configuration, and it is available at *https://colab.research.google.com/notebooks/welcome.ipynb*.

The Jupyter notebook is suitable for training simple models and testing ideas quickly. Google Colaboratory makes it easy to upload local files, install software in Jupyter notebooks, and even connect Google Colaboratory to a Jupyter runtime on your local machine.

Some of the supported features of Colaboratory include TF 2 execution with GPUs, visualization using Matplotlib, and the ability to save a copy of your Google Colaboratory notebook to Github by using `File > Save a copy to GitHub`.

Moreover, you can load any `.ipynb` on GitHub by just adding the path to the URL *colab.research.google.com/github/* (see the Colaboratory website for details).

Google Colaboratory has support for other technologies, such as HTML and SVG, enabling you to render SVG-based graphics in notebooks that are in Google Colaboratory. Remember that any software you install in a Google Colaboratory notebook is only available on a per-session basis: if you log out and log in again, you need to perform the same installation steps that you performed during your earlier Google Colaboratory session.

There is one other *very* nice feature of Google Colaboratory: you can execute code on a GPU for up to twelve hours per day for free. This free GPU support is extremely useful for people who do not have a suitable GPU on their local machine (which is probably the majority of users). Now, they can launch TF 2 code to train neural networks in less than 20 or 30 minutes, a process that would otherwise require multiple hours of CPU-based execution time.

You can launch Tensorboard inside a Google Colaboratory notebook with the following command (replace the specified directory with your own location):

```
%tensorboard --logdir /logs/images
```

Keep in mind the following details about Google Colaboratory. First, whenever you connect to a server in Google Colaboratory, you start a *session*.

You can execute the code in a session with a CPU (the default), GPU, or TPU (which is available for free), and you can execute your code without any time limit for your session. However, if you select the GPU option for your session, *only the first 12 hours of GPU execution time are free.* Any additional GPU time during that same session incurs a small charge (see the website for those details).

The other point to keep in mind is that any software that you install in a Jupyter notebook during a given session will *not* be saved when you exit that session. For example, the following code snippet installs `TFLearn` in a Jupyter notebook:

```
!pip install tflearn
```

When you exit the current session and later, start a new session, you need to install `TFLearn` again, as well as any other software (such as Github repositories) that you also installed in any previous session.

Incidentally, you can also run TF 2 code and TensorBoard in Google Colaboratory. Navigate to this URL for more information:

https://www.tensorflow.org/tensorboard/r2/tensorboard_in_notebooks

Uploading CSV Files in Google Colaboratory

Listing 2.25 displays the content `upload_csv_file.ipynb` that illustrates how to upload a CSV file in a Google Colaboratory notebook.

LISTING 2.25: upload_csv_file.ipynb

```
import pandas as pd

from google.colab import files
uploaded = files.upload()

df = pd.read_csv("weather_data.csv")
print("dataframe df:")
df
```

Listing 2.25 uploads the CSV file `weather_data.csv` whose contents are not shown because they are not important for this example. The code shown in bold is the Colaboratory-specific code that is required to upload the CSV file. When you launch this code, you will see a small button labeled "Browse," which you must click and then select the CSV file that is listed in the code snippet. After doing so, the rest of the code is executed and you will see the contents of the CSV file displayed in your browser session.

NOTE *You must supply the CSV file* `weather_data.csv` *if you want to launch this Jupyter notebook successfully in Google Colaboratory.*

SUMMARY

This chapter introduced you to the NumPy library for Python. You learned how to write Python scripts containing loops, arrays, and lists. You also saw how to work with dot products, the `reshape()` method, plotting with Matplotlib (discussed in more detail in Chapter 6), and examples of linear regression.

Then you learned how to work with subranges of arrays, and also negative subranges of vectors and arrays, both of which are very useful for extracting portions of datasets in machine learning tasks. You also saw various other NumPy operations, such as the `reshape()` method, which is useful when working with image files.

Next, you learned how to use NumPy for linear regression, the mean squared error (MSE), and how to calculate the MSE with the NumPy `linspace()` method. Finally, you had an introduction Google Colaboratory, where you can take advantage of the free GPU time when you launch Jupyter notebooks.

CHAPTER 3

Matplotlib and Visualization

This chapter introduces data visualization, along with a collection of Python-based code samples that use Matplotlib to render charts and graphs. In addition, this chapter contains visualization code samples that combine Pandas and Matplotlib.

The first part of this chapter briefly discusses data visualization, with a short list of some data visualization tools, and a list of various types of visualizations (bar graphs, pie charts, and so forth). Some introductory information can be found online:

https://medium.datadriveninvestor.com/dont-beat-the-bush-use-chatgpt-to-visualize-your-data-94cee442cc29

https://medium.datadriveninvestor.com/stop-wasting-times-to-learn-machine-learning-read-this-instead-5abfab230279

The first part of this chapter contains a short introduction to Matplotlib, followed by code samples that display the available colors in Matplotlib.

The second part of this chapter contains an assortment of Python code samples that render horizontal lines, slanted lines, and parallel lines. This section also contains a set of code samples that show you how to render a grid of points in several ways.

The third part of this chapter shows you how to load images, display a checkerboard pattern, and plot a trigonometric function in Matplotlib. The fourth section contains examples of rendering charts and graphs in Matplotlib, which includes histograms, bar charts, pie charts, and heat maps.

The final section contains code samples for rendering 3D charts, financial data, and data from a sqlite3 database.

WHAT IS DATA VISUALIZATION?

Data visualization refers to presenting data in a graphical manner, such as bar charts, line graphs, and heat maps. As you probably know, Big Data comprises massive amounts of data, which leverages data visualization tools to assist in making better decisions.

Data visualization is a crucial aspect of data analysis, providing an intuitive understanding of the underlying patterns and relationships. With tools like Matplotlib and Seaborn, Python has become an efficient platform for crafting compelling visuals. As always, the key lies in practice and exploration.

Visual representation of data enables viewers to quickly grasp complex data insights. Python, with its rich ecosystem of visualization libraries, provides tools to render data in meaningful ways. This chapter focuses on various visualization tasks using libraries such as Matplotlib and Seaborn.

Python is a versatile and powerful programming language that can be used for various applications ranging from Web development to data analysis. In this chapter, we will explore solutions to common programming tasks using Python. Each task will have a detailed explanation and solution.

Advanced visualization techniques offer deeper insights and more comprehensive narratives from data. Tools like Matplotlib and Seaborn make these tasks more accessible. While these visuals are powerful, it is essential to ensure clarity and avoid misrepresentation. Continue experimenting and refining your visualization skills to tell more compelling data stories.

In the realm of data visualization, the journey from novice to expert is marked by the adoption of advanced techniques that can extract and depict deeper insights from data. In this chapter, we will explore some of these advanced visualization techniques and understand how they can be applied to various data scenarios.

Effective data visualization is about conveying complex data narratives in an intuitive manner. As we continue our exploration, this chapter unfolds more advanced visualization techniques, enabling us to represent data in a multitude of insightful ways.

Good data visualization tells a meaningful story, focusing on useful information that resides in datasets that can contain many data points (i.e., billions of rows of data). Another aspect of data visualization is its effectiveness: how well does it convey the trends that might exist in the dataset?

There are many open source data visualization tools available, some of which are listed here (many others are available):

- Matplotlib
- Seaborn
- Bokeh
- YellowBrick
- Tableau
- D3.js (JavaScript and SVG)

In case you have not already done so, it would be helpful to install the following Python libraries (using `pip3`) on your computer so that you can launch the code samples in this chapter:

```
pip3 install matplotlib
pip3 install seaborn
pip3 install bokeh
```

Types of Data Visualization

Bar graphs, line graphs, and pie charts are common ways to present data, and yet many other types exist, some of which are listed here:

- 2D/3D Area Chart
- Bar Chart
- Gantt Chart
- Heat Map
- Histogram
- Polar Area
- Scatterplot (2D or 3D)
- Timeline

The Python code samples in the next several sections illustrate how to perform visualization via rudimentary APIs from Matplotlib.

WHAT IS MATPLOTLIB?

Matplotlib is a plotting library that supports NumPy, SciPy, and toolkits such as wxPython (among others). Matplotlib supports only version 3 of Python: support for version 2 of Python was available only through 2020. Matplotlib is a multi-platform library that is built on NumPy arrays.

The plotting-related code samples in this chapter use pyplot, which is a Matplotlib module that provides a MATLAB-like interface. Here is an example of using pyplot to plot a smooth curve based on negative powers of Euler's constant e:

```
import matplotlib.pyplot as plt
import numpy as np

a = np.linspace(0, 10, 100)
b = np.exp(-a)
plt.plot(a, b)
plt.show()
```

Keep in mind that the code samples that plot line segments assume that you are familiar with the equation of a (non-vertical) line in the plane: `y = m*x + b`, where `m` is the slope and `b` is the y-intercept.

Furthermore, some code samples use NumPy APIs, such as `np.linspace()`, `np.array()`, `np.random.rand()`, and `np.ones()`, which are discussed in Chapter 3, so you can refresh your memory regarding these APIs.

MATPLOTLIB STYLES

Listing 3.1 displays the content of `mpl_styles.py` that illustrates how to plot a pie chart in Matplotlib.

LISTING 3.1: mpl_styles.py

```
import matplotlib.pyplot as plt

print("plt.style.available:")
styles = plt.style.available

for style in styles:
  print("style:",style)
```

Listing 3.1 contains an `import` statement, followed by the variable `styles`, which is initialized with the set of available styles in Matplotlib. The final portion of Listing 3.1 contains a loop that iterates through the values in the `styles` variable. Launch the code in Listing 3.1, and you will see the following output:

```
plt.style.available:
style: Solarize_Light2
style: _classic_test_patch
style: bmh
style: classic
style: dark_background
style: fast
style: fivethirtyeight
style: ggplot
style: grayscale
style: seaborn
style: seaborn-bright
style: seaborn-colorblind
style: seaborn-dark
style: seaborn-dark-palette
style: seaborn-darkgrid
style: seaborn-deep
style: seaborn-muted
style: seaborn-notebook
style: seaborn-paper
style: seaborn-pastel
style: seaborn-poster
style: seaborn-talk
style: seaborn-ticks
style: sea born-white
style: seaborn-whitegrid
style: tableau-colorblind10
```

DISPLAY ATTRIBUTE VALUES

Listing 3.2 displays the content of `mat_attrib_values.py` that shows the attribute values of an object in Matplotlib (subplots are discussed later in this chapter).

LISTING 3.2: mat_attrib_values.py

```
import matplotlib.pyplot as plt

fig, ax = plt.subplots()

print("=> attribute values:")
print(plt.getp(fig))
```

Listing 3.2 contains an `import` statement, followed by the variables `fig` and `ax`, which are initialized by invoking the `subplots()` method of the `plt` class. The next block of code prints the attribute values in `fig` by invoking the `plt.getp()` method. Launch the code in Listing 3.2, and you will see the following output:

```
=> attribute values:
    agg_filter = None
    alpha = None
    animated = False
    axes = [<AxesSubplot:>]
    children = [<matplotlib.patches.Rectangle object at 
0x11c34f0...
    clip_box = None
    clip_on = True
    clip_path = None
    constrained_layout = False
    constrained_layout_pads = (0.04167, 0.04167, 0.02, 0.02)
    contains = None
    default_bbox_extra_artists = [<AxesSubplot:>, 
<matplotlib.spines.Spine object a...
    dpi = 100.0
    edgecolor = (1.0, 1.0, 1.0, 1.0)
    facecolor = (1.0, 1.0, 1.0, 1.0)
    figheight = 4.8
    figure = None
    figwidth = 6.4
    frameon = True
    gid = None
    in_layout = True
    label = 
    path_effects = []
    picker = None
    rasterized = None
    size_inches = [6.4 4.8]
    sketch_params = None
    snap = None
    tight_layout = False
    transform = IdentityTransform()
    transformed_clip_path_and_affine = (None, None)
```

```
    url = None
    visible = True
    window_extent = TransformedBbox(     Bbox(x0=0.0,
y0=0.0, x1=6.4, ...
    zorder = 0
None
```

COLOR VALUES IN MATPLOTLIB

Listing 3.3 displays the content of `mat_colors.py` that shows the colors that are available in Matplotlib.

LISTING 3.3: heatmap1.py

```
import matplotlib
import matplotlib.pyplot as plt

colors = plt.colormaps()

col_count=5
idx=0
for color in colors:
  if(color.endswith("_r") == False):
    print(color," ",end="")
    idx += 1
    if(idx % col_count == 0):
      print()
print()
print("=> color count:",idx)
```

Listing 3.3 contains two `import` statements, after which the variable `colors` are initialized with the list of available colors. The next portion of Listing 3.3 contains a loop that iterates through the `colors` variable, and prints the value of each color, provided that it does not have the suffix "_r" in its name. A new line is printed each time that five colors have been printed. Launch the code in Listing 3.3, and you will see the following output:

```
Accent  Blues  BrBG  BuGn  BuPu
CMRmap  Dark2  GnBu  Greens  Greys
OrRd  Oranges  PRGn  Paired  Pastel1
Pastel2  PiYG  PuBu  PuBuGn  PuOr
PuRd  Purples  RdBu  RdGy  RdPu
RdYlBu  RdYlGn  Reds  Set1  Set2
Set3  Spectral  Wistia  YlGn  YlGnBu
YlOrBr  YlOrRd  afmhot  autumn  binary
bone  brg  bwr  cividis  cool
coolwarm  copper  cubehelix  flag  gist_earth
gist_gray  gist_heat  gist_ncar  gist_rainbow  gist_stern
gist_yarg  gnuplot  gnuplot2  gray  hot
hsv  inferno  jet  magma  nipy_spectral
ocean  pink  plasma  prism  rainbow
seismic  spring  summer  tab10  tab20
tab20b  tab20c  terrain  turbo  twilight
twilight_shifted  viridis  winter
=> color count: 83
```

Now let's proceed to the next section that contains a fast-paced set of basic code samples that display various types of line segments.

CUBED NUMBERS IN MATPLOTLIB

Listing 3.4 displays the content of `cubed_numbers.py` that illustrates how to plot a set of points using Matplotlib.

LISTING 3.4: cubed_numbers.py

```
import matplotlib.pyplot as plt

plt.plot([1, 2, 3, 4], [1, 8, 27, 64])
plt.axis([0, 5, 0, 70])
plt.xlabel("Integers (1-4)")
plt.ylabel("Cubed Integers")
plt.show()
```

Listing 3.4 plots a set of integer-valued points whose x-coordinate is between 1 and 4, inclusive, and whose y-coordinate is the cube of the corresponding x-coordinate. The code sample also labels the horizontal axis and the vertical axis. Figure 3.1 displays these points in Listing 3.4.

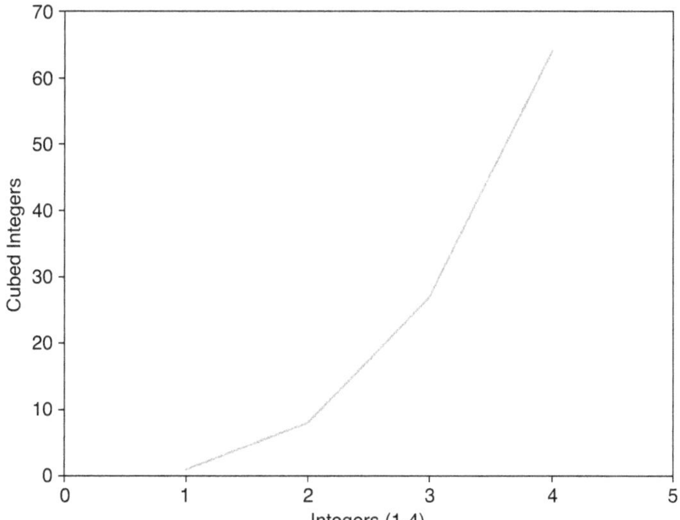

FIGURE 3.1 A graph of cubed numbers

HORIZONTAL LINES IN MATPLOTLIB

Listing 3.5 displays the content of `hlines1.py` that illustrates how to plot horizontal lines using Matplotlib. Recall that the equation of a non-vertical line in the 2D plane is `y = m*x + b`, where `m` is the slope of the line and `b` is the y-intercept of the line.

LISTING 3.5: hlines1.py

```
import numpy as np
import matplotlib.pyplot as plt

# top line
x1 = np.linspace(-5,5,num=200)
y1 = 4 + 0*x1

# middle line
x2 = np.linspace(-5,5,num=200)
y2 = 0 + 0*x2

# bottom line
x3 = np.linspace(-5,5,num=200)
y3 = -3 + 0*x3

plt.axis([-5, 5, -5, 5])
plt.plot(x1,y1)
plt.plot(x2,y2)
plt.plot(x3,y3)
plt.show()
```

Listing 3.5 uses the `np.linspace()` API to generate a list of 200 equally-spaced numbers for the horizontal axis, all of which are between -5 and 5. The three lines defined via the variables `y1`, `y2`, and `y3`, are defined in terms of the variables `x1`, `x2`, and `x3`, respectively.

Figure 3.2 displays three horizontal line segments whose equations are contained in Listing 3.5.

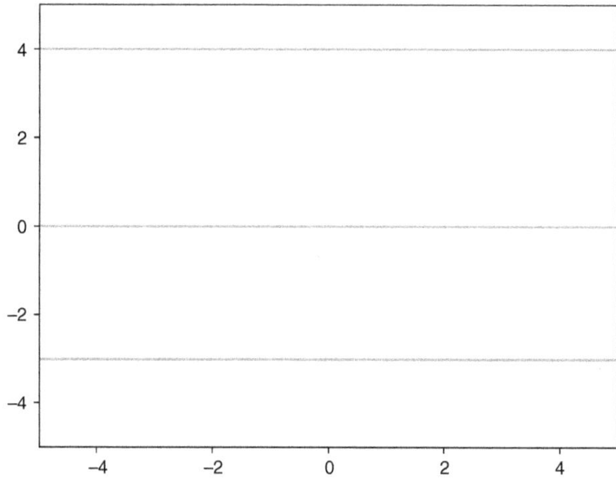

FIGURE 3.2 A graph of three horizontal line segments

SLANTED LINES IN MATPLOTLIB

Listing 3.6 displays the content of `diagonallines.py` that illustrates how to plot slanted lines.

LISTING 3.6: diagonallines.py

```
import matplotlib.pyplot as plt
import numpy as np

x1 = np.linspace(-5,5,num=200)
y1 = x1

x2 = np.linspace(-5,5,num=200)
y2 = -x2

plt.axis([-5, 5, -5, 5])
plt.plot(x1,y1)
plt.plot(x2,y2)
plt.show()
```

Listing 3.6 defines two lines using the technique that you saw in Listing 3.5, except that these two lines define `y1 = x1` and `y2 = -x2`, which produces slanted lines instead of horizontal lines.

Figure 3.3 displays two slanted line segments whose equations are defined in Listing 3.6.

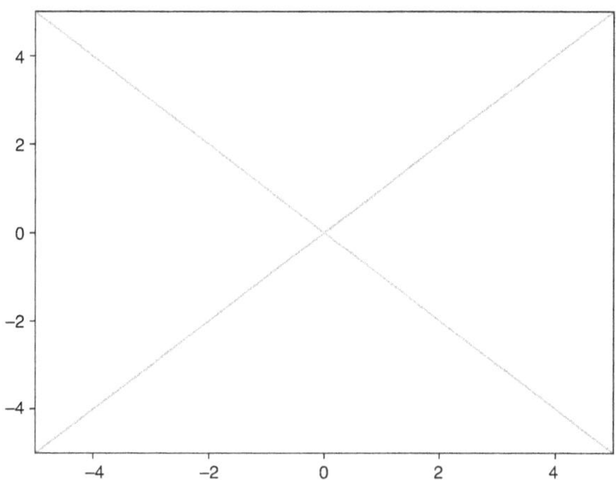

FIGURE 3.3 A graph of two slanted line segments

PARALLEL SLANTED LINES IN MATPLOTLIB

If two lines in the Euclidean plane have the same slope, then they are parallel. Listing 3.7 displays the content of `parallellines1.py` that illustrates how to plot parallel slanted lines.

LISTING 3.7: parallellines1.py

```
import matplotlib.pyplot as plt
import numpy as np

# lower line
x1 = np.linspace(-5,5,num=200)
y1 = 2*x1
```

```
# upper line
x2 = np.linspace(-5,5,num=200)
y2 = 2*x2 + 3

# horizontal axis
x3 = np.linspace(-5,5,num=200)
y3 = 0*x3 + 0

# vertical axis
plt.axvline(x=0.0)

plt.axis([-5, 5, -10, 10])
plt.plot(x1,y1)
plt.plot(x2,y2)
plt.plot(x3,y3)
plt.show()
```

Listing 3.7 defines three lines using the technique that you saw in Listing 3.6, where two lines are slanted and parallel, and the third line is horizontal. Launch the code in Listing 3.7, and you will see the result displayed in Figure 3.4.

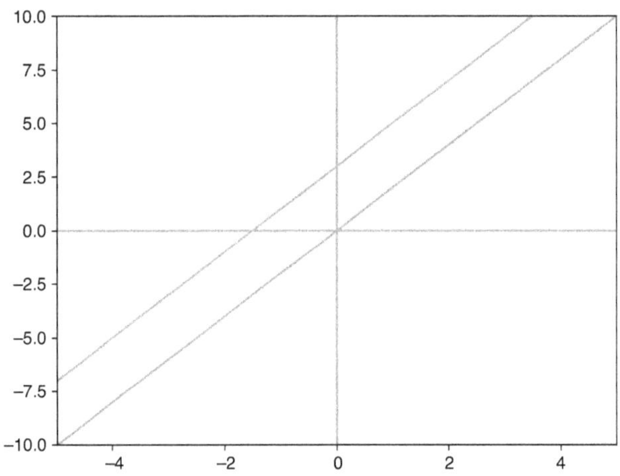

FIGURE 3.4 A graph of two slanted parallel line segments

A GRID OF POINTS IN MATPLOTLIB

Listing 3.8 displays the content of `plotgrid.py` that illustrates how to plot a simple grid.

LISTING 3.8: multi_lines.py

```
import matplotlib.pyplot as plt

x_coord = [ 50, 300, 175, 50]
y_coord = [ 50, 50,  150, 50]
plt.plot(x_coord,y_coord)
plt.scatter(x_coord,y_coord)
```

```
for x,y in zip(x_coord,y_coord):
  plt.text(x,y,'Coord ({x},{y})'.format(x=x,y=y))

x_coord = [ 175, 300,  50, 175]
y_coord = [  50, 150, 150, 50]
plt.plot(x_coord,y_coord)
plt.scatter(x_coord,y_coord)

for x,y in zip(x_coord,y_coord):
  plt.text(x,y,'Coord ({x},{y})'.format(x=x,y=y))
plt.show()
```

Listing 3.8 defines the NumPy variable `points` that defines a 2D list of points with three rows and four columns. The Pyplot API `plot()` uses the `points` variable to display a grid-like pattern. Figure 3.5 displays a grid of points, as defined in Listing 3.8.

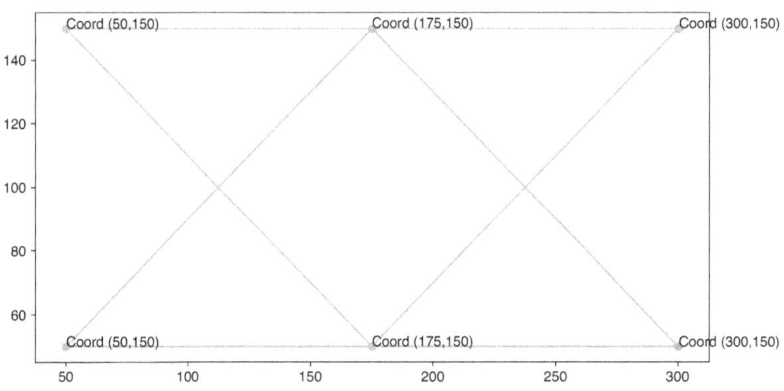

FIGURE 3.5 A grid of points generated by the code in Listing 3.8

A DOTTED GRID IN MATPLOTLIB

Listing 3.9 displays the content of `plotdottedgrid1.py` that illustrates how to plot a "dotted" grid pattern.

LISTING 3.9: plotdottedgrid1.py

```
import numpy as np
import pylab
from itertools import product
import matplotlib.pyplot as plt

fig = pylab.figure()
ax = fig.add_subplot(1,1,1)

ax.grid(which='major', axis='both', linestyle='--')

[line.set_zorder(3) for line in ax.lines]
fig.show() # to update

plt.gca().xaxis.grid(True)
plt.show()
```

Listing 3.9 is similar to the code in Listing 3.8 in that both of them plot a grid-like pattern; however, the former renders a "dotted" grid pattern whereas the latter renders a "dotted" grid pattern by specifying the value `'--'` for the `linestyle` parameter.

The next portion of Listing 3.9 invokes the `set_zorder()` method, that controls which items are displayed on top of other items, such as dots on top of lines, or vice versa. The final portion of Listing 3.9 invokes the `gca().xaxis.grid(True)` chained methods to display the vertical grid lines.

You can also use the `plt.style` directive to specify a style for figures. The following code snippet specifies the classic style of Matplotlib:

```
plt.style.use('classic')
```

Figure 3.6 displays a "dashed" grid pattern based on the code in Listing 3.9.

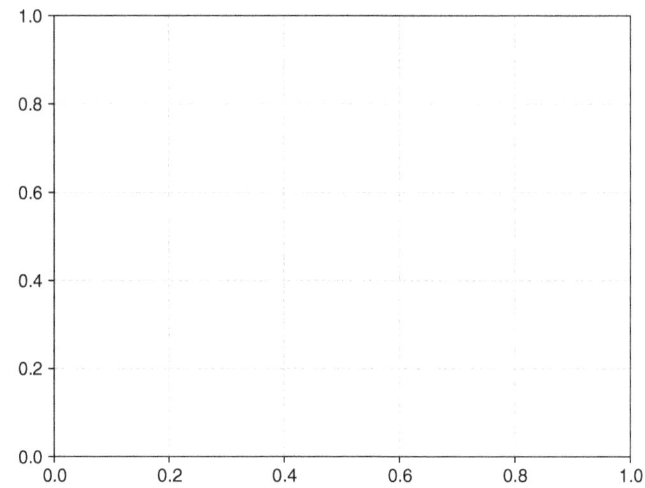

FIGURE 3.6 A "dashed" grid pattern generated using the code from Listing 3.9

TWO LINES AND A LEGEND IN MATPLOTLIB

Listing 3.10 displays the content of `plotgrid2.py` that illustrates how to display a colored grid.

LISTING 3.10: two_lines_legend.py

```
import matplotlib.pyplot as plt

# FIRST PLOT:
vals_x = [91,93,95,96,97,98,99,99,104,115]
vals_y = [1500,2000,3000,2500,1200,1500,2900,3200,5200,6500]
plt.plot(vals_x, vals_y) # alternate style
#plt.plot(vals_x, vals_y, label='First List')

# SECOND PLOT:
vals_x2 = [91,93,95,96,97,98,99,99,104,115]
```

```
vals_y2 = [1005,1006,1007,1008,1009,2031,3100,2033,3034,4035]
plt.plot(vals_x2, vals_y2)
#plt.plot(vals_x2, vals_y2, label='Second List') #
alternate style

# generate line plot:
plt.plot(vals_x, vals_y)
plt.title("Random Pairs of Numbers")
plt.xlabel("Random X Values")
plt.ylabel("Random Y Values")
plt.legend(['First List','Second List'])
#plt.legend() # alternate style
plt.show()
```

Listing 3.10 defines the NumPy variable data that defines a 2D set of points with ten rows and ten columns. The Pyplot API plot() uses the data variable to display two line graphs, as shown in Figure 3.7.

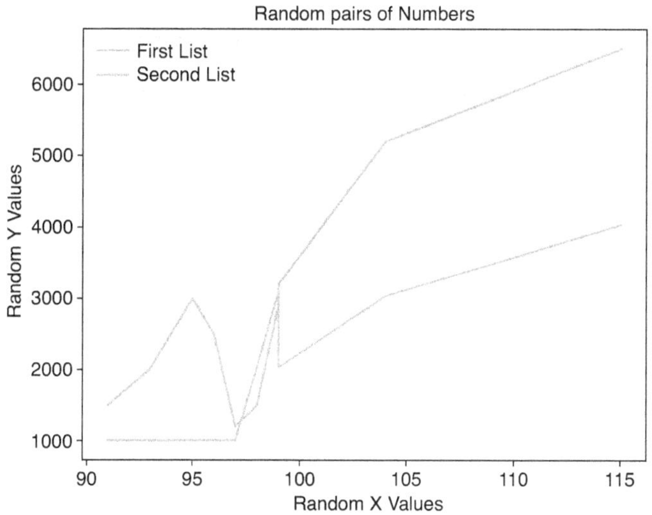

FIGURE 3.7 A pair of line segments

LOADING IMAGES IN MATPLOTLIB

Listing 3.11 displays the content of `load_images2.py` that illustrates how to display an image.

LISTING 3.11: load_images2.py

```
from sklearn.datasets import load_digits
from matplotlib import pyplot as plt

digits = load_digits()
```

```
#set interpolation='none'

fig = plt.figure(figsize=(3, 3))
plt.imshow(digits['images'][66], cmap="gray",
interpolation='none')
plt.show()
```

Listing 3.11 starts with two `import` statements, and then the `digits` variable is initialized with the contents of the `digits` dataset. The next portion of Listing 3.11 displays the contents of one of the images in the `digits` dataset. Launch the code in Listing 3.11, and you will see the image in Figure 3.8.

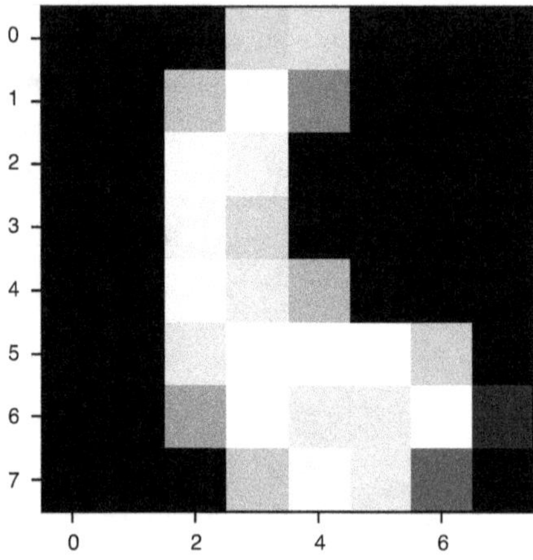

FIGURE 3.8 Loading an image in Matplotlib

A CHECKERBOARD IN MATPLOTLIB

Listing 3.12 displays the content of `checkerboard1.py` that illustrates how to display a checkerboard.

LISTING 3.12: checkerboard1.py

```
import matplotlib.pyplot as plt
from matplotlib import colors
import numpy as np

data = np.random.rand(10, 10) * 20

# create discrete colormap
cmap = colors.ListedColormap(['red', 'blue'])
bounds = [0,10,20]
norm = colors.BoundaryNorm(bounds, cmap.N)

fig, ax = plt.subplots()
ax.imshow(data, cmap=cmap, norm=norm)

# draw gridlines
```

```
ax.grid(which='major', axis='both', linestyle='-',
color='k', linewidth=2)
ax.set_xticks(np.arange(-.5, 10, 1));
ax.set_yticks(np.arange(-.5, 10, 1));

plt.show()
```

Listing 3.12 defines the NumPy variable `data` that defines a 2D set of points with ten rows and ten columns. The Pyplot API `plot()` uses the `data` variable to display a colored grid-like pattern. Figure 3.9 displays a colored grid whose equations are contained in Listing 3.12.

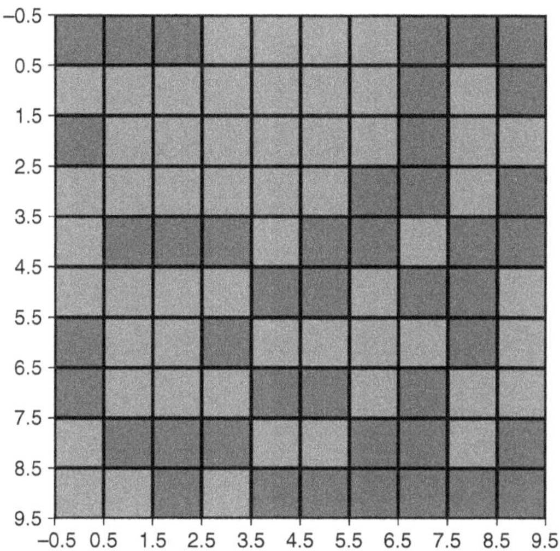

FIGURE 3.9 A checkerboard generated by Matplotlib

RANDOMIZED DATA POINTS IN MATPLOTLIB

Listing 3.13 displays the content of `lin_reg_plot.py` that illustrates how to plot a graph of random points.

LISTING 3.13: lin_plot_reg.py

```
import numpy as np
import matplotlib.pyplot as plt

trX = np.linspace(-1, 1, 101) # Linear space of 101 and [-1,1]

#Create the y function based on the x axis
trY = 2*trX + np.random.randn(*trX.shape)*0.4+0.2

#create figure and scatter plot of the random points
plt.figure()
plt.scatter(trX,trY)

# Draw one line with the line function
```

```
plt.plot (trX, .2 + 2 * trX)
plt.show()
```

Listing 3.13 defines the NumPy variable `trX` that contains 101 equally spaced numbers that are between -1 and 1 (inclusive). The variable `trY` is defined in two parts: the first part is `2*trX` and the second part is a random value that is partially based on the length of the one-dimensional array `trX`. The variable `trY` is the sum of these two "parts," which creates a "fuzzy" line segment.

The next portion of Listing 3.13 creates a scatterplot based on the values in `trX` and `trY`, followed by the Pyplot API `plot()` that renders a line segment. Figure 3.10 displays a random set of points based on the code in Listing 3.13.

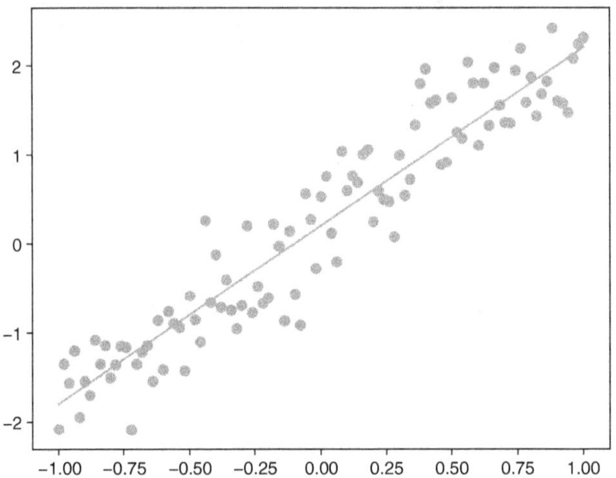

FIGURE 3.10 A random set of points based on the code in Listing 3.13

A SET OF LINE SEGMENTS IN MATPLOTLIB

Listing 3.14 displays the content of `line_segments.py` that illustrates how to plot a set of connected line segments in Matplotlib.

LISTING 3.14: line_segments.py

```
import numpy as np
import matplotlib.pyplot as plt

x = [7,11,13,15,17,19,23,29,31,37]

plt.plot(x) # OR: plt.plot(x, 'ro-') or bo
plt.ylabel('Height')
plt.xlabel('Weight')
plt.show()
```

Listing 3.14 defines the array `x` that contains a hard-coded set of values. The Pyplot API `plot()` uses the variable `x` to display a set of connected line segments. Figure 3.11 displays the result of launching the code in Listing 3.14.

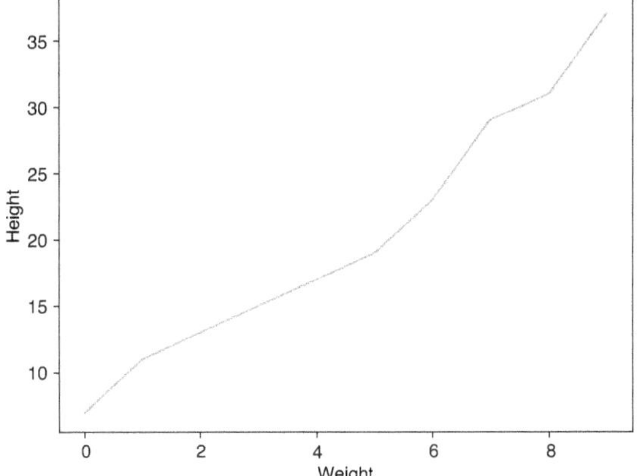

FIGURE 3.11 A set of connected line segments

PLOTTING MULTIPLE LINES IN MATPLOTLIB

Listing 3.15 displays the content of `plt_array2.py` that illustrates the ease with which you can plot multiple lines in Matplotlib.

LISTING 3.15: plt_array2.py

```
import matplotlib.pyplot as plt

x = [7,11,13,15,17,19,23,29,31,37]
data = [[8, 4, 1], [5, 3, 3], [6, 0, 2], [1, 7, 9]]
plt.plot(data, 'd-')
plt.show()
```

Listing 3.15 defines the array `data` that contains a hard-coded set of values. The Pyplot API `plot()` uses the variable `data` to display a line segment. Figure 3.12 displays multiple lines based on the code in Listing 3.15.

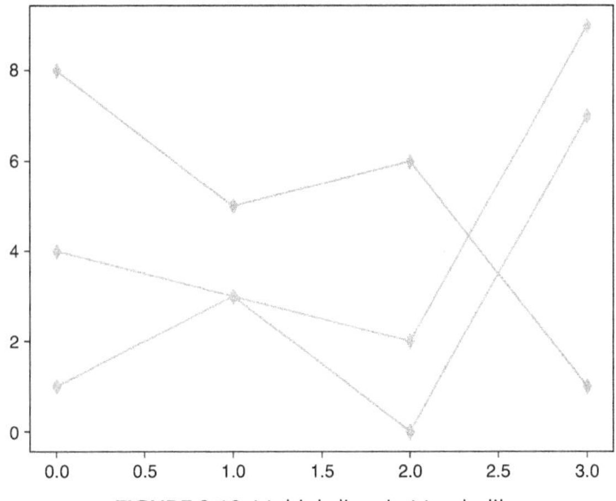

FIGURE 3.12 Multiple lines in Matplotlib

TRIGONOMETRIC FUNCTIONS IN MATPLOTLIB

You can display the graph of trigonometric functions as easily as you can render "regular" graphs using Matplotlib. Listing 3.16 displays the content of `sincos.py` that illustrates how to plot a sine function and a cosine function in Matplotlib.

LISTING 3.16: sincos.py

```
import numpy as np
import math

x = np.linspace(0, 2*math.pi, 101)
s = np.sin(x)
c = np.cos(x)

import matplotlib.pyplot as plt
plt.plot (s)
plt.plot (c)
plt.show()
```

Listing 3.16 defines the NumPy variables `x`, `s`, and `c` using the NumPy APIs `linspace()`, `sin()`, and `cos()`, respectively. Next, the Pyplot API `plot()` uses these variables to display a sine function and a cosine function.

Figure 3.13 displays a graph of two trigonometric functions based on the code in Listing 3.16.

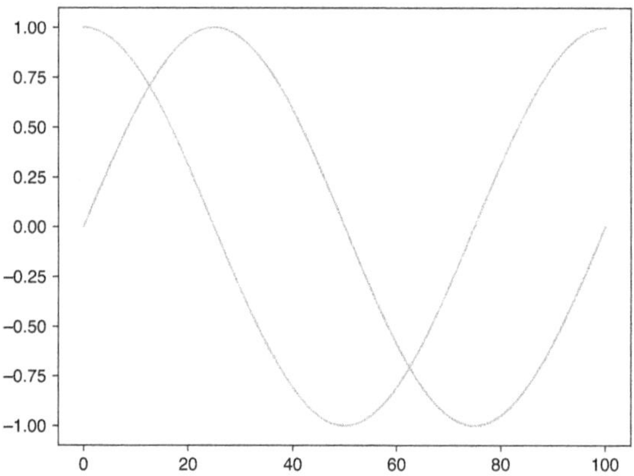

FIGURE 3.13 Sine and cosine trigonometric functions

Now let's look at a simple dataset consisting of discrete data points, which is the topic of the next section.

A HISTOGRAM IN MATPLOTLIB

Listing 3.17 displays the content of `histogram1.py` that illustrates how to plot a histogram using Matplotlib.

LISTING 3.17: histogram1.py

```
import matplotlib.pyplot as plt

x = [1, 2, 3, 4, 5, 6, 7, 4]

plt.hist(x, bins = [1, 2, 3, 4, 5, 6, 7])
plt.title("Histogram")
plt.legend(["bar"])
plt.show()
```

Listing 3.17 is straightforward: the variable x is initialized as a set of numbers, followed by a block of code that renders a histogram based on the data in the variable x. Launch the code in Listing 3.17, and you will see the histogram that is shown in Figure 3.14.

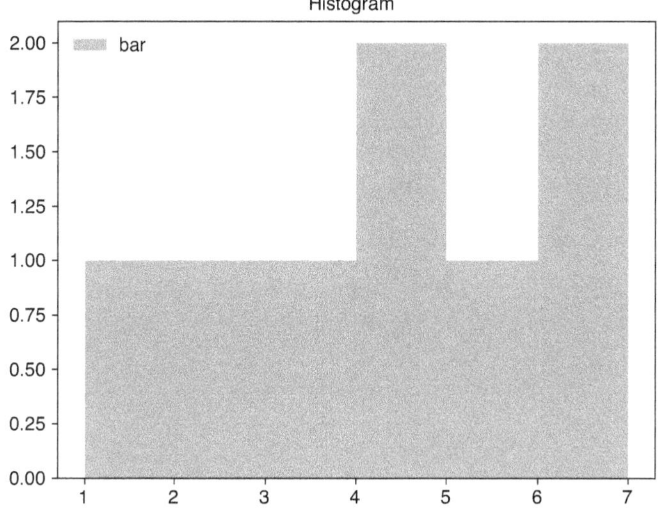

FIGURE 3.14 A histogram based on random values

HISTOGRAM WITH DATA FROM A SQLITE3 TABLE

Listing 3.18 displays the content of `rainfall_hist2.py` that shows you how to define a simple SQL query to create a histogram based on the data from the rainfall table.

LISTING 3.18: rainfall_hist3.py

```
import sqlite3
import pandas as pd
import matplotlib.pyplot as plt

sql = """
  SELECT
  cast(centimeters/5.00 as int)*5 as cent_floor,
  count(*) as count
```

```
FROM rainfall
GROUP by 1
ORDER by 1;
"""

con = sqlite3.connect("mytools.db")
df = pd.read_sql_query(sql, con)
con.close()

print("=> Histogram of Rainfall:")
print(df)

#df.hist(column='count', bins=7, grid=False, rwidth=1.0,
color='red')
df.hist(column='count', bins=14, grid=False, rwidth=.8,
color='red')
plt.show()
```

Listing 3.18 starts with several `import` statements and then initializes the variable `sql` with a SQL statement that selects data from the `rainfall` table. The next portion of Listing 3.18 initializes the variable `con` for accessing the `mytools.db` database, and then populates the Pandas data frame `df` with the result of executing the SQL statement contained in the variable `sql`. Now launch the code in Listing 3.18, and you will see the following output:

```
=> Histogram of Rainfall:
   bucket_floor    bucket_name  count
0             0   FROM 0 TO 10     27
1            10  FROM 10 TO 20     14
2            20  FROM 20 TO 30      9
3            30  FROM 30 TO 40      9
4            40  FROM 40 TO 50      3
5            50  FROM 50 TO 60      2
6            60  FROM 60 TO 70      1
```

The histogram that is shown in Figure 3.15 was created from this data.

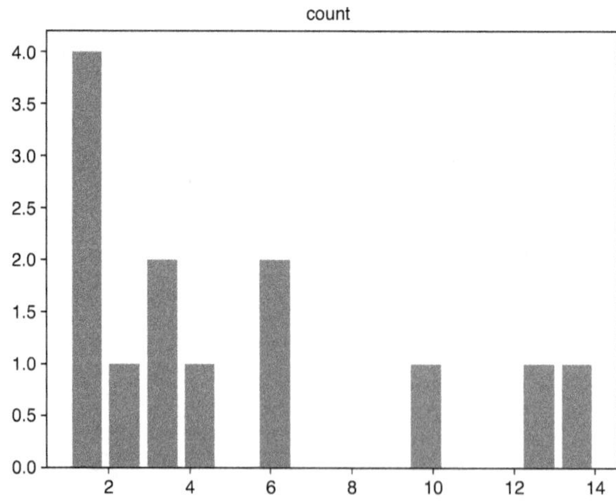

FIGURE 3.15 A histogram based on rainfall data

PLOT BAR CHARTS IN MATPLOTLIB

Listing 3.19 displays the content of `barchart1.py` that illustrates how to plot a bar chart in Matplotlib.

LISTING 3.19: barchart1.py

```
import matplotlib.pyplot as plt

x = [3, 1, 3, 12, 2, 4, 4]
y = [3, 2, 1, 4, 5, 6, 7]

plt.bar(x, y)

plt.title("Bar Chart")
plt.legend(["bar"])
plt.show()
```

Listing 3.19 contains an `import` statement followed by the variables `x` and `y` that are initialized as a list of numbers. Next, the bar chart is generated by invoking the `bar()` method of the `plt` class. The final block of code sets the title and legend for the bar chart and then displays the bar chart. Launch the code in Listing 3.19, and you will see the pie chart displayed in Figure 3.16.

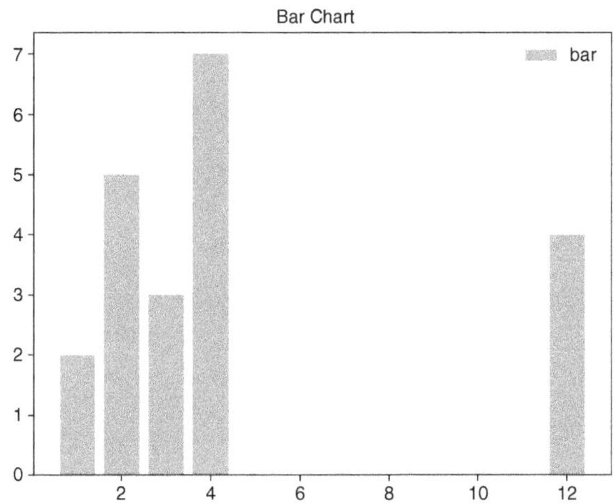

FIGURE 3.16 A bar chart using Matplotlib

Listing 3.20 displays the content of `barchart2.py` that illustrates how to plot a bar chart in Matplotlib.

LISTING 3.20: barchart2.py

```
import matplotlib.pyplot as plt

plt.bar([0.25,1.25,2.25,3.25,4.25],
        [50,40,70,80,20],
        label="GDP1",width=.5)
```

```
plt.bar([.75,1.75,2.75,3.75,4.75],
        [80,20,20,50,60],
        label="GDP2", color='r',width=.5)

plt.legend()
plt.xlabel('Months')
plt.ylabel('GDP (Billion Euross)')
plt.title('Bar Chart Comparison')
```

Listing 3.20 contains an `import` statement followed by the definition of two bar charts that are displayed in a side-by-side manner. Notice that the definition of each bar chart involves specifying the `x` and `y` (even though they are not explicitly included), followed by a value for the `label` and `width` arguments. The final block of code sets the legend and labels for the horizontal and vertical axes. Launch the code in Listing 3.20, and you will see the bar charts shown in Figure 3.17.

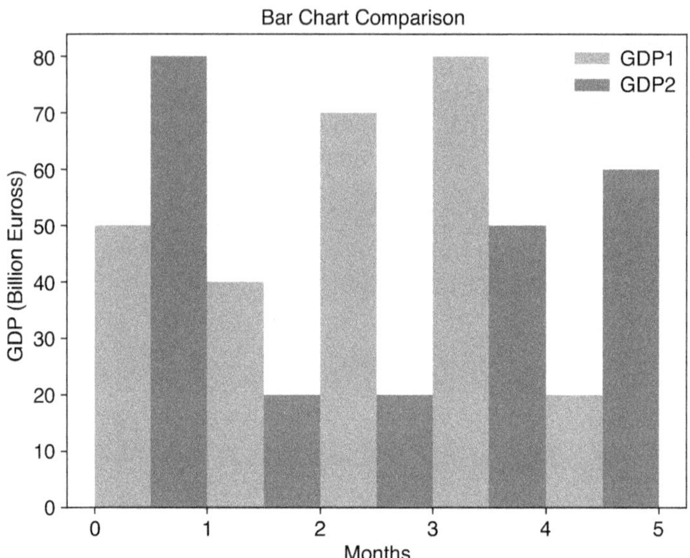

FIGURE 3.17 Two bar charts generated by the code in Listing 3.20

PLOT A PIE CHART IN MATPLOTLIB

Listing 3.21 displays the content of `piechart1.py` that illustrates how to plot a pie chart in Matplotlib.

LISTING 3.21: piechart1.py

```
import numpy as np

# data to display on plots
x = [1, 2, 3, 4]

# explode the first wedge:
e =(0.1, 0, 0, 0)
```

```
plt.pie(x, explode = e)
plt.title("Pie chart")
plt.show()
```

Listing 3.21 contains an `import` statement followed by the variables `x` and `e` that are initialized as a list of numbers. The values for `x` are used to calculate the relative size of each "slice" of the pie chart, and the values for the variable `e` indicate that the first pie slice is "exploded" slightly (indicated by the value 0.1 in `e`). Launch the code in Listing 3.21, and you will see the pie chart displayed in Figure 3.18.

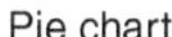

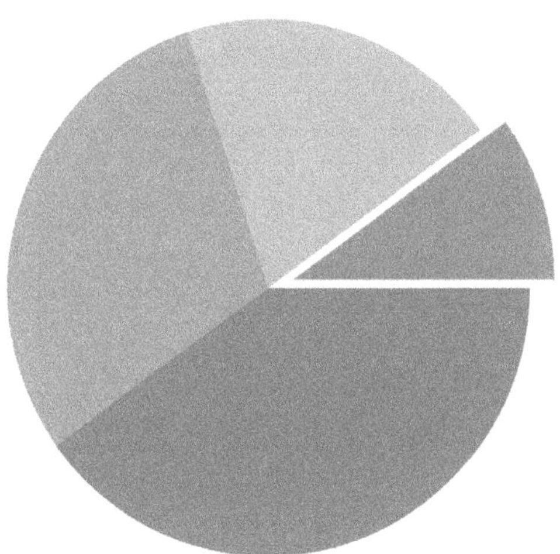

FIGURE 3.18 A pie chart generated by the code in Listing 3.21

HEAT MAPS IN MATPLOTLIB

Listing 3.22 displays the content of `heatmap1.py` that illustrates how to render a heat map in Matplotlib.

LISTING 3.22: heatmap1.py

```
import numpy as np

data = np.random.random((16, 16))
plt.imshow(data, cmap='tab20_r', interpolation='nearest')
plt.show()
```

Listing 3.22 contains an `import` statement, followed by the variable `data` that is initialized as a 16x16 matrix of random values. The next code snippet renders the heat map, and the final code snippet displays the heatmap. Launch the code in Listing 3.22, and you will see the image that is shown in Figure 3.19.

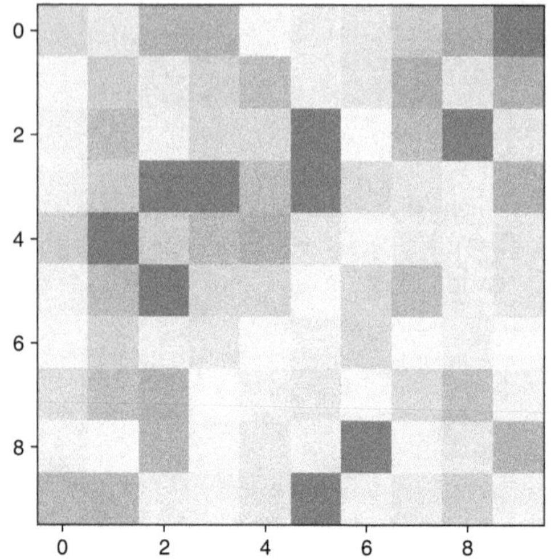

FIGURE 3.19 A heat map generated by the code in Listing 3.22

SAVE PLOT AS A PNG FILE

Listing 3.23 displays the content of `matplot2png.py` that shows you how to save a graphics image as a PNG file.

LISTING 3.23: matplot2png.py

```
import matplotlib.pyplot as plt
import numpy as np

outfile="graph1.png"

plt.figure()
plt.plot(range(6))

fig, ax = plt.subplots()

ax.plot([2, 3, 4, 5, 5, 6, 6],
        [5, 7, 1, 3, 4, 6 ,8])

ax.plot([1, 2, 3, 4, 5],
        [2, 3, 4, 5, 6])

x = np.linspace(0, 12, 100)
plt.plot(np.sin(x))
plt.plot(np.linspace(-4,4,50))

plt.savefig(outfile, dpi=300)
```

Listing 3.23 contains `import` statements, followed by the variable `outfile`, which is initialized with the name of the PNG file that will be saved to the file system. The contents of the PNG file consist of a sine wave and a set of line segments. Launch the code in Listing 3.23, and you will see the image that is shown in Figure 3.20.

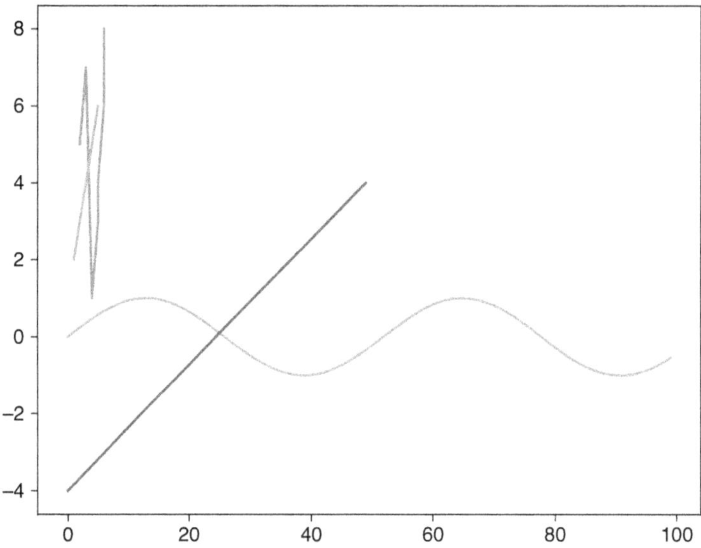

FIGURE 3.20 A heat map generated with the code from Listing 3.23

WORKING WITH SWEETVIZ

`SweetViz` is an open source Python module that generates remarkably detailed visualizations in the form of HTML Web pages based on five lines of Python code.

As a simple illustration, Listing 3.24 shows the content of `sweetviz1.py` that generates a visualization of various aspects of the `Iris` dataset that is available in Scikit-learn.

LISTING 3.24: sweetviz1.py

```
import sweetviz as sv
import seaborn as sns

df = sns.load_dataset('iris')
report = sv.analyze(df)
report.show_html()
```

Listing 3.24 starts with two `import` statements, followed by an initialization of the variable `df` with the contents of the `Iris` dataset. The next code snippet initializes the variable report as the result of invoking the `analyze()` method in `SweetViz`, followed by a code snippet that generates an HTML Web page with the result of the analysis.

Launch the code from the command line, and you will see a new HTML Web page called `SWEETVIZ_REPORT.html` in the same directory. Figure 3.21 displays the contents of the Web page `SWEETVIZ_REPORT.html`.

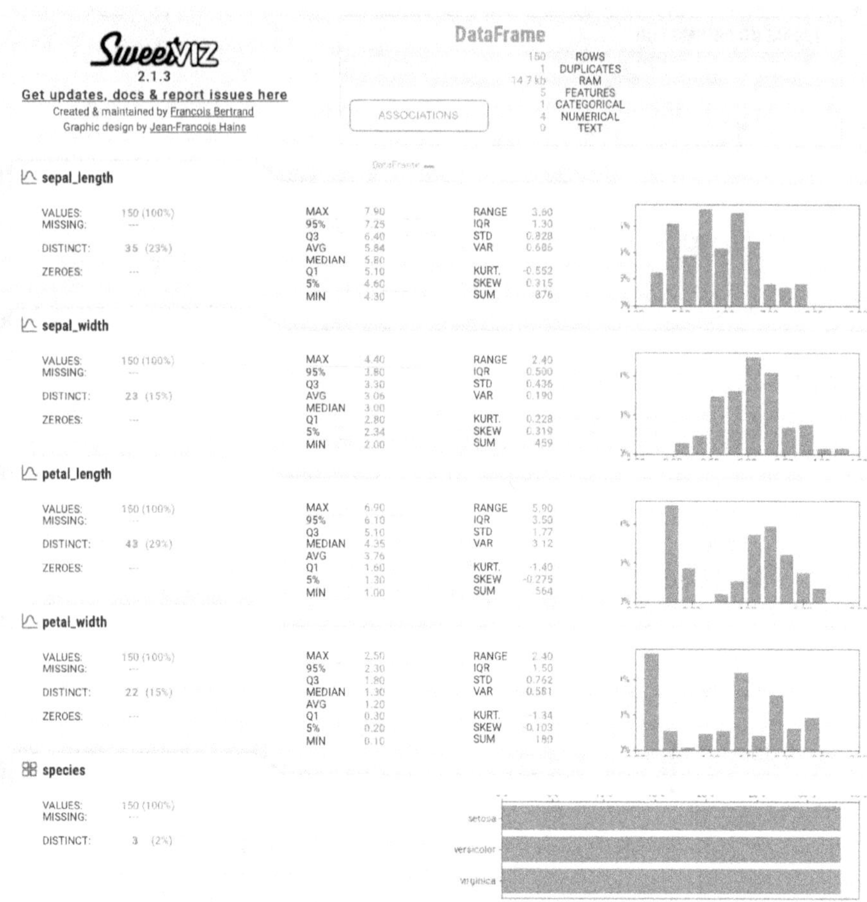

FIGURE 3.21 An analysis of the Iris dataset

WORKING WITH SKIMPY

`Skimpy` is an open-source Python module that generates an analysis of a dataset directly from the command line: no Python code is required. Install `Skimpy` with the following command:

```
pip3 install skimpy
```

Launch the following command to analyze the `Titanic` dataset (or a dataset of your own choice) and redirects the output to a text file (the latter is optional):

```
skimpy titanic.csv >titanic_out.txt
```

Figure 3.22 displays the contents of the generated output from the preceding command.

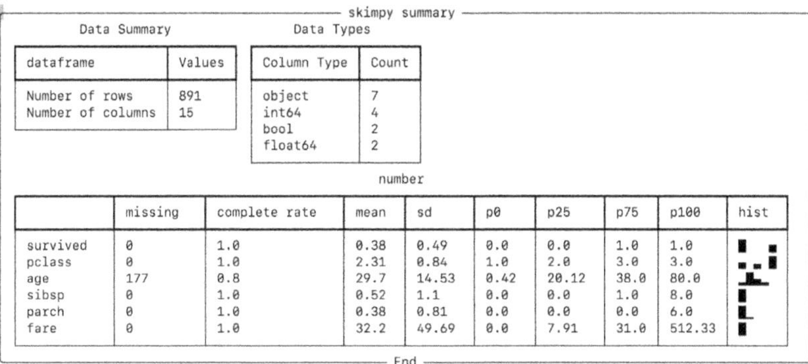

skimpy summary

Data Summary

dataframe	Values
Number of rows	891
Number of columns	15

Data Types

Column Type	Count
object	7
int64	4
bool	2
float64	2

number

	missing	complete rate	mean	sd	p0	p25	p75	p100	hist
survived	0	1.0	0.38	0.49	0.0	0.0	1.0	1.0	
pclass	0	1.0	2.31	0.84	1.0	2.0	3.0	3.0	
age	177	0.8	29.7	14.53	0.42	20.12	38.0	80.0	
sibsp	0	1.0	0.52	1.1	0.0	0.0	1.0	8.0	
parch	0	1.0	0.38	0.81	0.0	0.0	0.0	6.0	
fare	0	1.0	32.2	49.69	0.0	7.91	31.0	512.33	

End

FIGURE 3.22 An analysis of the Titanic dataset

3D CHARTS IN MATPLOTLIB

Listing 3.25 displays the content of `matplot_3d.py` that illustrates how to render a 3D plot in Matplotlib.

LISTING 3.25: matplot_3d.py

```
import matplotlib.pyplot as plt
import numpy as np

zline = np.linspace(0,40,1000)
xline = 2*np.sin(2*zline)
yline = 3*np.cos(3*zline)

ax = plt.axes(projection="3d")
ax.plot3D(xline,yline,zline,'red',linewidth=4)
plt.show()
```

Listing 3.25 contains `import` statements, followed by the variables `zline`, `xline`, and `yline` that are initialized via the NumPy methods `linspace()`, `sin()`, and `cos()`, respectively. The next portion of Listing 3.25 initializes the variable `ax` in order to display a 3D effort, which is rendered by the final code snippet. Launch the code in Listing 3.25, and you will see the image that is shown in Figure 3.23.

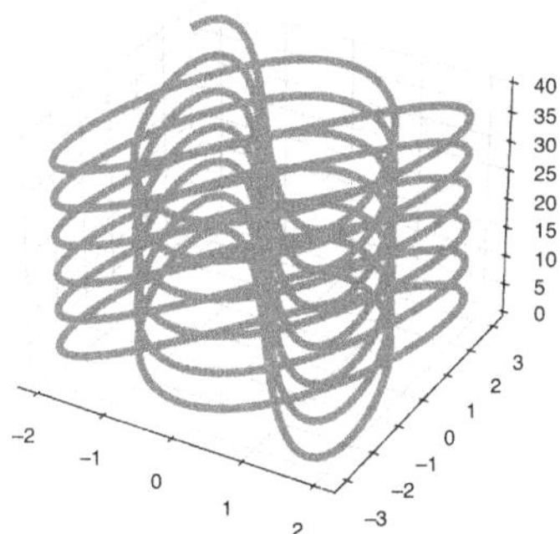

FIGURE 3.23 A 3D plot

PLOTTING FINANCIAL DATA WITH MPLFINANCE

The section contains a Python-based code sample that shows you how to plot financial data for a given stock. First, make sure that you have the necessary Python library installed, as shown here:

```
pip3 install mplfinance
```

Listing 3.26 displays the content of `financial_mpl.py` that illustrates how to plot financial data in Matplotlib.

LISTING 3.26: financial_mpl.py

```
#optional:
import sys
sys.path.append('/usr/local/lib/python3.9/site-packages')

import matplotlib.pyplot as plt
import pandas as pd

csvfile="aapl.csv"
daily = pd.read_csv(csvfile,index_col=0,parse_dates=True)
daily.index.name = 'Date'

print("daily.head():")
print(daily.head())
print()

print("daily.tail():")
print(daily.tail())

import mplfinance as mpf
mpf.plot(daily)

#Plot types: ohlc, candle, line, renko, and pnf
```

Listing 3.26 contains `import` statements, followed by the variable `csvfile` that contains AAPL data for the years 2017 and 2018. Next, the variable `daily` is initialized with the contents of `aapl.csv`, followed by a block of code that prints the first 5 lines and the final 5 lines of data in `aapl.csv`.

The final code snippet invokes the `plot()` method of the class `mpf` (which is imported from `mplfinance`) in order to render a chart. Launch the code in Listing 3.26, and you will see the following output:

```
daily.head():
                  Open        High  ...   Adj Close    Volume
Date                                ...
2017-01-03  115.800003  116.330002  ...  114.311760  28781900
2017-01-04  115.849998  116.510002  ...  114.183815  21118100
2017-01-05  115.919998  116.860001  ...  114.764473  22193600
2017-01-06  116.779999  118.160004  ...  116.043915  31751900
2017-01-09  117.949997  119.430000  ...  117.106812  33561900

[5 rows x 6 columns]
```

```
daily.tail():
                    Open        High  ...   Adj Close    Volume
Date                                  ...
2018-01-12  176.179993  177.360001  ...  177.089996  25418100
2018-01-16  177.899994  179.389999  ...  176.190002  29565900
2018-01-17  176.149994  179.250000  ...  179.100006  34386800
2018-01-18  179.369995  180.100006  ...  179.259995  31193400
2018-01-19  178.610001  179.580002  ...  178.460007  31269600

[5 rows x 6 columns]
```

Figure 3.24 displays a plot of financial data based on the code in Listing 3.29.

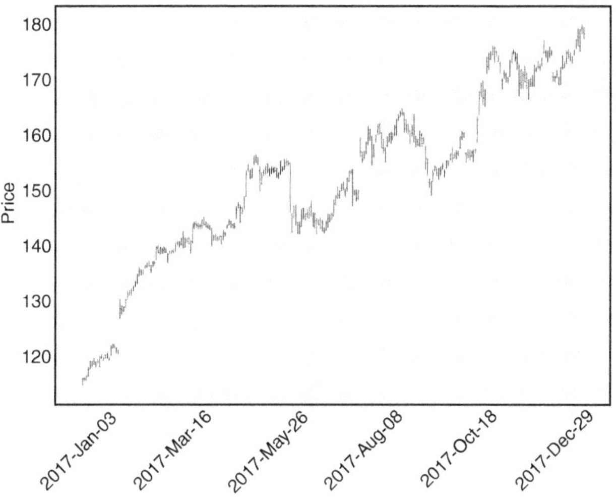

FIGURE 3.24 Plot of financial data for years 2017 and 2018

CHARTS AND GRAPHS WITH DATA FROM SQLITE3

Listing 3.27 displays the content of `rainfall_multiple.py` that shows you how to generate multiple charts and graphs from data that is extracted from a `sqlite3` database.

LISTING 3.27: rainfall_multiple.py

```
import sqlite3
import pandas as pd
import matplotlib.pyplot as plt

sql = """
  SELECT
  cast(centimeters/5.00 as int)*5 as cent_floor,
  count(*) as count
FROM rainfall
GROUP by 1
ORDER by 1;
```

```
"""

con = sqlite3.connect("mytools.db")
df = pd.read_sql_query(sql, con)
con.close()

####################################
# generate 7 types of charts/graphs
# and save them as PNG or TIFF files
####################################
df.hist(column='count', bins=14, grid=False, rwidth=.8,
color='red')
plt.savefig("rainfall_histogram.tiff")

df.plot.pie(y='count',figsize=(8,6))
plt.savefig("rainfall_pie.png")

df.plot.line(y='count',figsize=(8,6))
plt.savefig("rainfall_line.png")

df.plot.scatter(y='count',x='cent_floor',figsize=(8,6))
plt.savefig("rainfall_scatter.png")

df.plot.box(figsize=(8,6))
plt.savefig("rainfall_box.png")

df.plot.hexbin(x='count', y='cent_floor',gridsize=30,
figsize=(8,6))
plt.savefig("rainfall_hexbin.png")
df["cent_floor"].plot.kde()
plt.savefig("rainfall_kde.png")

df["count"].hist()
df.plot.line(x='count', y='cent_floor', figsize=(8,6))
df.plot.scatter(x='count', y='cent_floor', figsize=(8,6))
df.plot.box(figsize=(8,6))
df.plot.hexbin(x='count', y='cent_floor',gridsize=30,
figsize=(8,6))
df.plot.pie(y='cost', figsize=(8, 6))
df["cent_floor"].plot.kde()
```

Listing 3.27 contains several `import` statements and then initializes the variable `sql` with a SQL statement that selects data from the `rainfall` table. The next portion of Listing 3.27 initializes the variable `con` for accessing the `mytools.db` database, and then populates the Pandas data frame `df` with the result of executing the SQL statement contained in the variable `sql`.

The next portion of Listing 3.27 contains pairs of code snippets for rendering charts and graphs of various types (histogram, pie, line, scatter, box, hexbin, and kde). Launch the code in Listing 3.27, and you will see the following output:

```
=> Histogram of Rainfall:
   cent_floor  count
```

```
0              0     14
1              5     13
2             10      4
3             15     10
4             20      3
5             25      6
6             30      3
7             35      6
8             40      2
9             45      1
10            50      1
11            55      1
12            60      1
```

In addition to the preceding output, you will also see the following files in the same directory where you launched the code in Listing 3.27:

```
rainfall_histogram.tiff
rainfall_pie.png
rainfall_line.png
rainfall_scatter.png
rainfall_box.png
rainfall_hexbin.png
rainfall_kde.png
```

SUMMARY

This chapter started with a very short introduction to Matplotlib, along with code samples that displayed the available colors in Matplotlib.

Then you learned how to render horizontal lines, slanted lines, parallel lines, and a grid of points. In addition, you learned how to load images, display checkerboard patterns, and plot trigonometric functions. You also saw how to render histograms, bar charts, pie charts, and heat maps.

Next, you saw how to create a 3D plot, as well as how to render financial data and a chart with data from a sqlite3 database.

CHAPTER 4

SEABORN FOR DATA VISUALIZATION

This chapter introduces several tools for data visualization, including `Seaborn` and `Bokeh`. This chapter also contains a gentle introduction to `Scikit-learn` (which is typically imported as `sklearn`).

The first part of the chapter introduces you to `Seaborn` for data visualization, which is a layer above `Matplotlib`. Although `Seaborn` does not have all of the features that are available in `Matplotlib`, `Seaborn` provides an easier set of APIs for rendering charts and graphs.

The second portion of this chapter contains a very short introduction to `Bokeh`, along with a code sample that illustrates how to create a more artistic graphics effect with relative ease in `Bokeh`.

The third part of the chapter introduces you to `Scikit-learn`, which is a very powerful `Python` library that supports many machine learning algorithms and also supports visualization. If you are new to machine learning, fear not: *this section does not require a background in machine learning in order to understand the Python code samples.*

WORKING WITH SEABORN

`Seaborn` is a `Python` library for data visualization that also provides a high-level interface to `Matplotlib`. `Seaborn` is easier to work with than `Matplotlib`, and actually extends `Matplotlib`, but keep in mind that `Seaborn` is not as powerful as `Matplotlib`.

`Seaborn` addresses two challenges of `Matplotlib`. The first involves the default `Matplotlib` parameters. `Seaborn` works with different parameters, which provides greater flexibility than the default rendering of `Matplotlib` plots. `Seaborn` addresses the limitations of the `Matplotlib` default values for features such as colors, tick marks on the upper and right axes, and the style (among others).

In addition, Seaborn makes it easier to plot entire data frames (somewhat like Pandas) than doing so in Matplotlib. Nevertheless, since Seaborn extends Matplotlib, knowledge of the latter is advantageous and will simplify your learning curve.

Features of Seaborn

Seaborn provides a nice set of features and useful methods to control the display of data, some of which are listed here:

- scale Seaborn plots
- set the plot style
- set the figure size
- rotate label text
- set xlim or ylim
- set log scale
- add titles

Some useful Seaborn methods are listed here:

- plt.xlabel()
- plt.ylabel()
- plt.annotate()
- plt.legend()
- plt.ylim()
- plt.savefig()

Seaborn supports various built-in datasets, just like NumPy and Pandas, including the Iris dataset and the Titanic dataset, both of which you will see in subsequent sections. As a starting point, the next section contains the code that displays all the available built-in datasets in Seaborn.

SEABORN DATASET NAMES

Listing 4.1 displays the contents dataset_names.py that displays the Seaborn built-in datasets, one of which we will use in a subsequent section in order to render a heat map in Seaborn.

LISTING 4.1: dataset_names.py

```
import seaborn as sns

names = sns.get_dataset_names()
for name in names:
  print("name:",name)
```

Listing 4.1 contains an `import` statement and then the variable `names` that is initialized with the set of built-in dataset names in `Seaborn`. The next portion contains a loop that iterates through the dataset names in the variable `names` and displays their values. Launch the code in Listing 4.1 and you will see the following output:

```
name: anagrams
name: anscombe
name: attention
name: brain_networks
name: car_crashes
name: diamonds
name: dots
name: exercise
name: flights
name: fmri
name: gammas
name: geyser
name: iris
name: mpg
name: penguins
name: planets
name: taxis
name: tips
name: titanic
```

The three-line code sample in the next section shows you how to display the rows in the built-in "tips" dataset.

SEABORN BUILT-IN DATASETS

Listing 4.2 displays the contents of `seaborn_tips.py` that illustrates how to read the `tips` dataset into a data frame and display the first five rows of the dataset.

LISTING 4.2: seaborn_tips.py

```
import seaborn as sns

df = sns.load_dataset("tips")
print(df.head())
```

Listing 4.2 is very simple: after importing `seaborn`, the variable `df` is initialized with the data in the built-in dataset `tips`, and the `print()` statement displays the first five rows of `df`. Note that the `load_dataset()` API searches for online or built-in datasets. The output from Listing 4.2 is here:

```
   total_bill   tip     sex smoker  day    time  size
0       16.99  1.01  Female     No  Sun  Dinner     2
1       10.34  1.66    Male     No  Sun  Dinner     3
```

```
2         21.01  3.50    Male     No  Sun  Dinner     3
3         23.68  3.31    Male     No  Sun  Dinner     2
4         24.59  3.61  Female     No  Sun  Dinner     4
```

THE IRIS DATASET IN SEABORN

Listing 4.3 displays the contents of `seaborn_iris.py` that illustrates how to plot the `Iris` dataset.

LISTING 4.2: seaborn_iris.py

```
import seaborn as sns
import matplotlib.pyplot as plt

# Load iris data
iris = sns.load_dataset("iris")

# Construct iris plot
sns.swarmplot(x="species", y="petal_length", data=iris)

# Show plot
plt.show()
```

Listing 4.3 imports `Seaborn` and `matplotlib.pyplot` and then initializes the variable `iris` with the contents of the built-in `Iris` dataset. Next, the `swamplot()` API displays a graph with the horizontal axis labeled `species`, the vertical axis labeled `petal_length`, and the displayed points are from the `Iris` dataset.

Figure 4.1 displays the images in the `Iris` dataset based on the code in Listing 4.3.

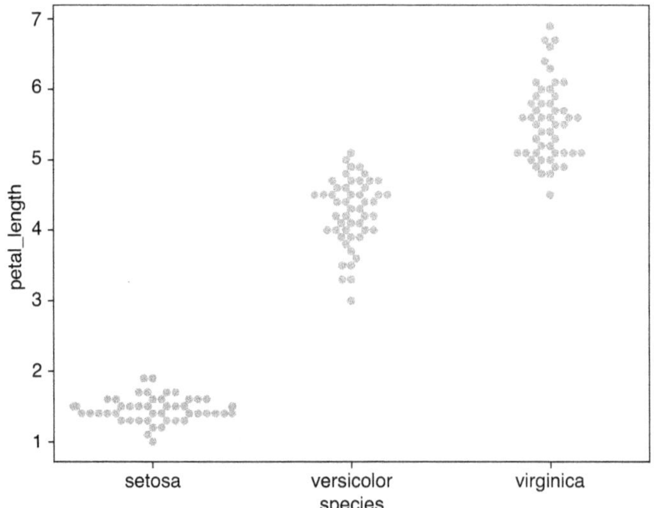

FIGURE 4.1 The Iris dataset.

THE TITANIC DATASET IN SEABORN

Listing 4.4 displays the contents of `seaborn_titanic_plot.py` that illustrates how to plot the `Titanic` dataset.

LISTING 4.4: seaborn_titanic_plot.py

```
import matplotlib.pyplot as plt
import seaborn as sns

titanic = sns.load_dataset("titanic")
g = sns.factorplot("class", "survived", "sex",
data=titanic, kind="bar", palette="muted", legend=False)

plt.show()
```

Listing 4.4 contains the same `import` statements as Listing 4.3, and then initializes the variable `titanic` with the contents of the built-in `Titanic` dataset. Next, the `factorplot()` API displays a graph with dataset attributes that are listed in the API invocation. Figure 4.2 displays a plot of the data in the `Titanic` dataset based on the code in Listing 4.4.

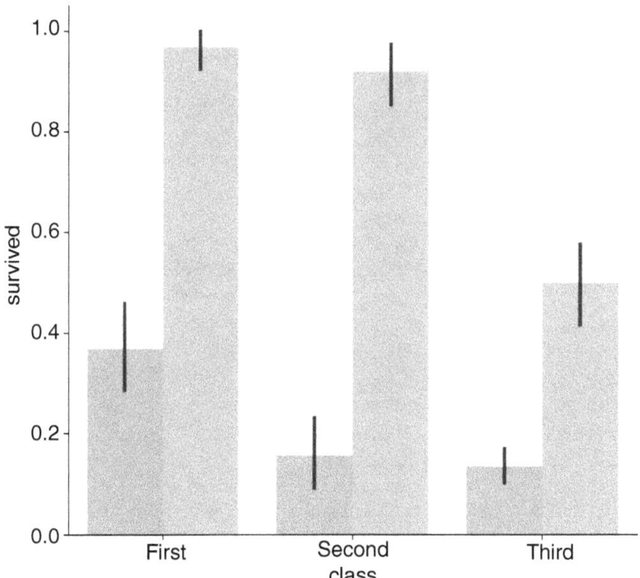

FIGURE 4.2 A histogram of the Titanic dataset.

EXTRACTING DATA FROM TITANIC DATASET IN SEABORN (1)

Listing 4.5 displays the contents of `seaborn_titanic.py` that illustrates how to extract subsets of data from the `Titanic` dataset.

LISTING 4.5: seaborn_titanic.py

```
import matplotlib.pyplot as plt
import seaborn as sns

titanic = sns.load_dataset("titanic")
print("titanic info:")
titanic.info()

print("first five rows of titanic:")
print(titanic.head())

print("first four ages:")
print(titanic.loc[0:3,'age'])

print("fifth passenger:")
print(titanic.iloc[4])

#print("first five ages:")
#print(titanic['age'].head())

#print("first five ages and gender:")
#print(titanic[['age','sex']].head())

#print("descending ages:")
#print(titanic.sort_values('age', ascending = False).head())

#print("older than 50:")
#print(titanic[titanic['age'] > 50])

#print("embarked (unique):")
#print(titanic['embarked'].unique())

#print("survivor counts:")
#print(titanic['survived'].value_counts())

#print("counts per class:")
#print(titanic['pclass'].value_counts())

#print("max/min/mean/median ages:")
#print(titanic['age'].max())
#print(titanic['age'].min())
#print(titanic['age'].mean())
#print(titanic['age'].median())
```

Listing 4.5 contains the same `import` statements as Listing 4.4, and then initializes the variable `titanic` with the contents of the built-in `Titanic` dataset. The next portion of Listing 4.5 displays various aspects of the `Titanic` dataset, such as its structure, the first five rows, the first four ages, and the details of the fifth passenger.

As you can see, there is a large block of "commented out" code that you can uncomment in order to see the associated output, such as age, gender, persons over 50, unique rows, and so forth. The output from Listing 4.5 is here:

```
#print(titanic['age'].mean())
titanic info:
<class 'pandas.core.frame.Data frame'>
RangeIndex: 891 entries, 0 to 890
Data columns (total 15 columns):
survived       891 non-null int64
pclass         891 non-null int64
sex            891 non-null object
age            714 non-null float64
sibsp          891 non-null int64
parch          891 non-null int64
fare           891 non-null float64
embarked       889 non-null object
class          891 non-null category
who            891 non-null object
adult_male     891 non-null bool
deck           203 non-null category
embark_town    889 non-null object
alive          891 non-null object
alone          891 non-null bool
dtypes: bool(2), category(2), float64(2), int64(4), object(5)
memory usage: 80.6+ KB
first five rows of titanic:
   survived  pclass     sex   age  sibsp  parch     fare embarked  class \
0         0       3    male  22.0      1      0   7.2500        S  Third
1         1       1  female  38.0      1      0  71.2833        C  First
2         1       3  female  26.0      0      0   7.9250        S  Third
3         1       1  female  35.0      1      0  53.1000        S  First
4         0       3    male  35.0      0      0   8.0500        S  Third

     who  adult_male deck  embark_town alive  alone
0    man        True  NaN  Southampton    no  False
1  woman       False    C    Cherbourg   yes  False
2  woman       False  NaN  Southampton   yes   True
3  woman       False    C  Southampton   yes  False
4    man        True  NaN  Southampton    no   True
first four ages:
0    22.0
1    38.0
2    26.0
3    35.0
Name: age, dtype: float64
fifth passenger:
survived                 0
pclass                   3
sex                   male
age                     35
sibsp                    0
parch                    0
fare                  8.05
embarked                 S
class                Third
who                    man
adult_male            True
deck                   NaN
embark_town    Southampton
alive                   no
alone                 True
Name: 4, dtype: object
counts per class:
```

```
3    491
1    216
2    184
Name: pclass, dtype: int64
max/min/mean/median ages:
80.0
0.42
29.69911764705882
28.0
```

EXTRACTING DATA FROM TITANIC DATASET IN Seaborn (2)

Listing 4.6 displays the contents of `seaborn_titanic2.py` that illustrates how to extract subsets of data from the `Titanic` dataset.

LISTING 4.6: seaborn_titanic2.py

```
import matplotlib.pyplot as plt
import seaborn as sns

titanic = sns.load_dataset("titanic")

# Returns a scalar
# titanic.ix[4, 'age']
print("age:",titanic.at[4, 'age'])

# Returns a Series of name 'age', and the age values
associated
# to the index labels 4 and 5
# titanic.ix[[4, 5], 'age']
print("series:",titanic.loc[[4, 5], 'age'])

# Returns a Series of name '4', and the age and fare values
# associated to that row.
# titanic.ix[4, ['age', 'fare']]
print("series:",titanic.loc[4, ['age', 'fare']])

# Returns a Data frame with rows 4 and 5, and columns 'age'
and 'fare'
# titanic.ix[[4, 5], ['age', 'fare']]
print("data frame:",titanic.loc[[4, 5], ['age', 'fare']])

query = titanic[
    (titanic.sex == 'female')
    & (titanic['class'].isin(['First', 'Third']))
    & (titanic.age > 30)
    & (titanic.survived == 0)
]
print("query:",query)
```

Listing 4.6 contains the same `import` statements as Listing 4.5, and then initializes the variable `titanic` with the contents of the built-in `Titanic` dataset. The next code snippet displays the age of the passenger with index 4 in the dataset (which equals 35).

The following code snippet displays the ages of passengers with index values 4 and 5 in the dataset:

```
print("series:",titanic.loc[[4, 5], 'age'])
```

The next snippet displays the age and fare of the passenger with index 4 in the dataset, followed by another code snippet displays the age and fare of the passengers with index 4 and index 5 in the dataset.

The final portion of Listing 4.6 is the most interesting part: it defines a variable `query` as shown here:

```
query = titanic[
    (titanic.sex == 'female')
    & (titanic['class'].isin(['First', 'Third']))
    & (titanic.age > 30)
    & (titanic.survived == 0)
]
```

The preceding code block will retrieve the female passengers who are in either first class or third class, and who are also over 30, and who did not survive the accident. The entire output from Listing 4.6 is here:

```
age: 35.0
series: 4    35.0
5      NaN
Name: age, dtype: float64
series: age       35
fare    8.05
Name: 4, dtype: object
data frame:      age    fare
4  35.0  8.0500
5   NaN  8.4583
query:      survived  pclass     sex   age  sibsp  parch     fare embarked
class  \
18             0       3  female  31.0      1      0  18.0000        S  Third
40             0       3  female  40.0      1      0   9.4750        S  Third
132            0       3  female  47.0      1      0  14.5000        S  Third
167            0       3  female  45.0      1      4  27.9000        S  Third
177            0       1  female  50.0      0      0  28.7125        C  First
254            0       3  female  41.0      0      2  20.2125        S  Third
276            0       3  female  45.0      0      0   7.7500        S  Third
362            0       3  female  45.0      0      1  14.4542        C  Third
396            0       3  female  31.0      0      0   7.8542        S  Third
```

```
503      0      3  female  37.0      0      0   9.5875      S  Third
610      0      3  female  39.0      1      5  31.2750      S  Third
638      0      3  female  41.0      0      5  39.6875      S  Third
657      0      3  female  32.0      1      1  15.5000      Q  Third
678      0      3  female  43.0      1      6  46.9000      S  Third
736      0      3  female  48.0      1      3  34.3750      S  Third
767      0      3  female  30.5      0      0   7.7500      Q  Third
885      0      3  female  39.0      0      5  29.1250      Q  Third
```

VISUALIZING A PANDAS DATASET IN SEABORN

Listing 4.7 displays the contents of `pandas_seaborn.py` that illustrates how to display a `Pandas` dataset in `Seaborn`.

LISTING 4.7: pandas_seaborn.py

```
import pandas as pd
import random
import matplotlib.pyplot as plt
import seaborn as sns

df = pd.Data frame()

df['x'] = random.sample(range(1, 100), 25)
df['y'] = random.sample(range(1, 100), 25)

print("top five elements:")
print(df.head())

# display a density plot
#sns.kdeplot(df.y)

# display a density plot
#sns.kdeplot(df.y, df.x)

#sns.distplot(df.x)

# display a histogram
#plt.hist(df.x, alpha=.3)
#sns.rugplot(df.x)

# display a boxplot
#sns.boxplot([df.y, df.x])

# display a violin plot
#sns.violinplot([df.y, df.x])

# display a heatmap
#sns.heatmap([df.y, df.x], annot=True, fmt="d")

# display a cluster map
#sns.clustermap(df)
```

```
# display a scatterplot of the data points
sns.lmplot('x', 'y', data=df, fit_reg=False)
plt.show()
```

Listing 4.7 contains several familiar `import` statements, followed by the initialization of the `Pandas` variable `df` as a `Pandas` DataFrame. The next two code snippets initialize the columns and rows of the dataframe and the `print()` statement display the first five rows.

For your convenience, Listing 4.7 contains an assortment of "commented out" code snippets that use `Seaborn` in order to render a density plot, a histogram, a boxplot, a violin plot, a heatmap, and a cluster. Uncomment the portions that interest you in order to see the associated plot. The output from Listing 4.7 is here:

```
top five elements:
    x   y
0  52  34
1  31  47
2  23  18
3  34  70
4  71   1
```

Figure 4.3 displays a plot of the data in the `Titanic` dataset based on the code in Listing 4.7.

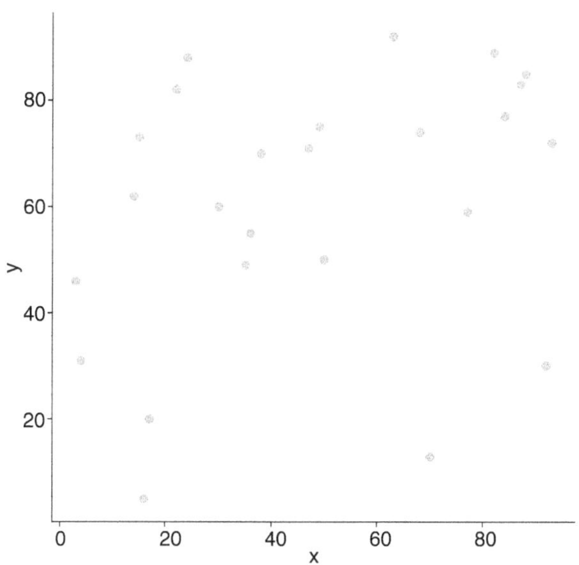

FIGURE 4.3 A Pandas DataFrame displayed via `Seaborn`.

SEABORN HEAT MAPS

Listing 4.8 displays the contents `heatmap1.py` that displays a heat map from a `Seaborn` built-in dataset.

LISTING 4.8: heatmap1.py

```
import seaborn as sns
import matplotlib.pyplot as plt

data = sns.load_dataset("flights")
data = data.pivot("month", "year", "passengers")

print("data.head():")
print(data.head())

sns.heatmap(data)
plt.show()
```

Listing 4.8 contains two `import` statements, followed by the variable data that is initialized with the contents of the `Seaborn` built-in dataset called `flights`. The next code snippet invokes the `pivot()` method that selects the attributes month, year, and passengers from the dataset. The next portion of code displays the first five rows of the dataset, followed by a code block that renders a heat map and you will see the following output:

```
data.head():
year   1949  1950  1951  1952  1953  1954  1955  1956  1957  1958  1959  1960
month
Jan     112   115   145   171   196   204   242   284   315   340   360   417
Feb     118   126   150   180   196   188   233   277   301   318   342   391
Mar     132   141   178   193   236   235   267   317   356   362   406   419
Apr     129   135   163   181   235   227   269   313   348   348   396   461
May     121   125   172   183   229   234   270   318   355   363   420   472
```

Figure 4.4 displays a heat map plot of the data in the `flights` dataset based on the code in Listing 4.8.

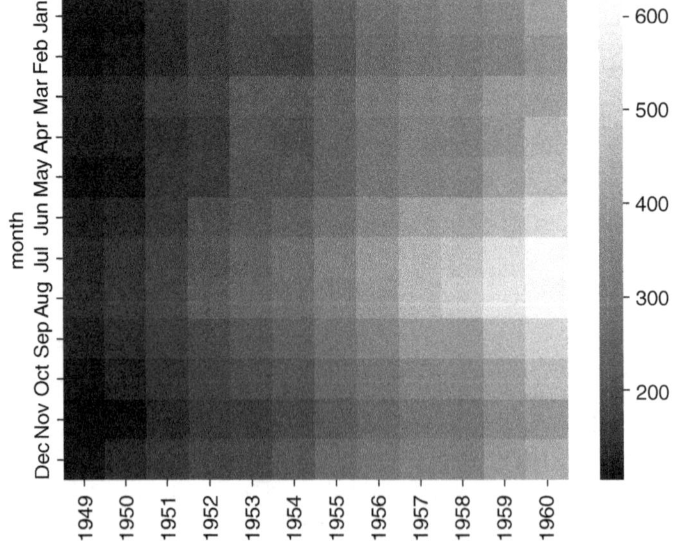

FIGURE 4.4 A `Pandas` DataFrame displayed as a `Seaborn` heat map.

SEABORN PAIR PLOTS

This section contains several `Python`-based code samples that show you how to use the `Seaborn pair_plot()` method to render pair plots.

Listing 4.9 displays the contents `seborn_pairplot1.py` that displays a pair plot with the `Iris` dataset.

LISTING 4.9: seaborn_pairplot1.py

```
import seaborn as sns
import pandas as pd
import matplotlib.pyplot as plt

# load iris data
iris = sns.load_dataset("iris")

df = pd.Data frame(iris)

# construct and display iris plot
g = sns.pairplot(df, height=2, aspect=1.0)
plt.show()
```

Listing 4.9 starts with `import` statements, followed by the variable `iris` that is initialized with the contents of the `Seaborn` built-in dataset called `iris`. The next code snippet initializes the variable df with the contents of the dataset. The final block of code generates a pair plot based on the contents of the variable df, and then displays the pair plot. Figure 4.5 displays a plot of the data in the `iris` dataset based on the code in Listing 4.9.

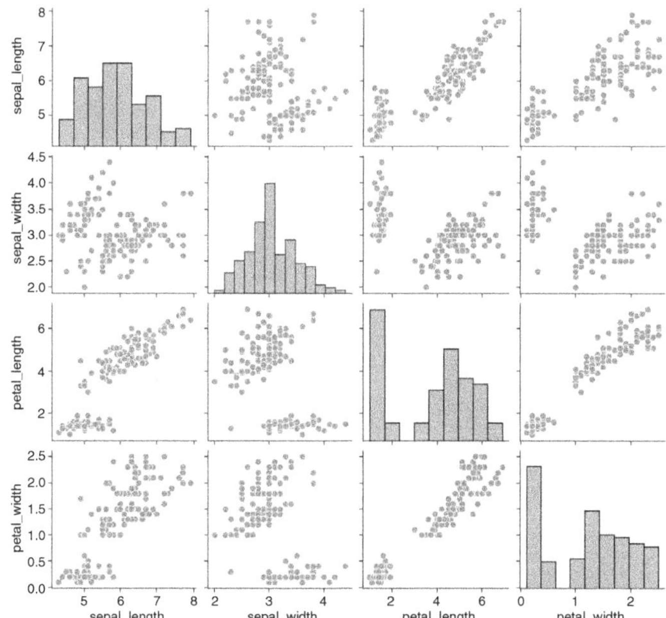

FIGURE 4.5 A `Seaborn` pair plot.

Listing 4.10 displays the contents seborn_pairplot12.py that renders a pair plot with the Iris dataset.

LISTING 4.10: seaborn_pairplot2.py

```
import seaborn as sns
import pandas as pd
import matplotlib.pyplot as plt

# load iris data
iris = sns.load_dataset("iris")

df = pd.Data frame(iris)

# IRIS columns:
# sepal_length,sepal_width,petal_length,petal_width,species

# plot a subset of columns:
plot_columns = ['sepal_length', 'sepal_width']
sns.pairplot(df[plot_columns])
plt.show()

# specify KDE for the diagonal:
sns.pairplot(df[plot_columns], diag_kind='kde')
plt.show()
```

Listing 4.10 starts with the same code as Listing 4.9, followed by the variable plot_columns that contains sepal-related attributes from the iris dataset. The next code block generates a pair plot and displays its contents, followed by a code snippet that generates a pair plot with the argument diag_kind equal to kde.

Figure 4.6 displays a pair plot of the data in the iris dataset based on the code in Listing 4.10.

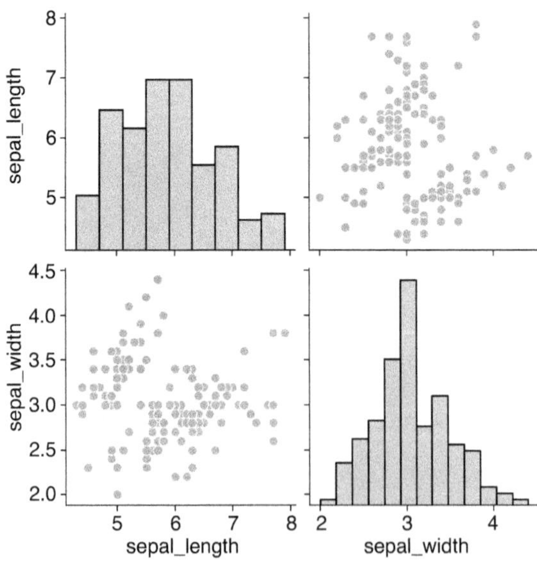

FIGURE 4.6 A Seaborn pair plot of Iris data.

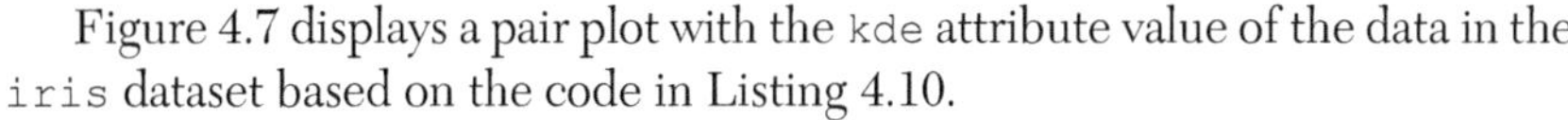

Figure 4.7 displays a pair plot with the `kde` attribute value of the data in the `iris` dataset based on the code in Listing 4.10.

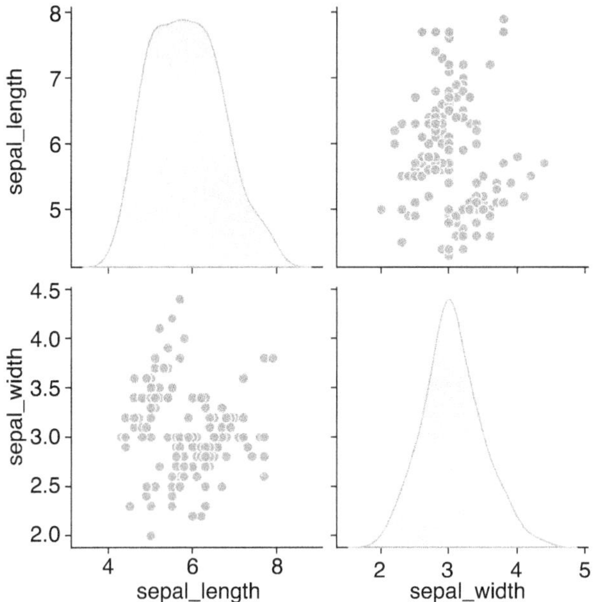

FIGURE 4.7 A Seaborn pair plot of Iris data with kde option.

WHAT IS BOKEH?

`Bokeh` is an open source project that depends on `Matplotlib` as well as `Scikit-learn`. As you will see in the subsequent code sample, `Bokeh` generates an HTML Web page that is based on `Python` code, and then launches that Web page in a browser. `Bokeh` and `D3.js` (which is a JavaScript layer of abstraction over `SVG`) both provide elegant visualization effects that support animation effects and user interaction.

`Bokeh` enables the rapid creation statistical visualization, and it works with other tools with as `Python` Flask and Django. In addition to `Python`, `Bokeh` supports Julia, Lua, and R (`JSON` files are generated instead of HTML Web pages).

Listing 4.11 displays the contents `bokeh_trig.py` that illustrates how to create a graphics effect using various `Bokeh` APIs.

LISTING 4.11: bokeh_trig.py

```
# pip3 install bokeh
from bokeh.plotting import figure, output_file, show
from bokeh.layouts import column
import bokeh.colors as colors
import numpy as np
import math
```

```
deltaY = 0.01
maxCount = 150
width  = 800
height = 400
band_width = maxCount/3

x = np.arange(0, math.pi*3, 0.05)
y1 = np.sin(x)
y2 = np.cos(x)

white = colors.RGB(255,255,255)

fig1 = figure(plot_width = width, plot_height = height)

for i in range(0,maxCount):
  rgb1 = colors.RGB(i*255/maxCount, 0, 0)
  rgb2 = colors.RGB(i*255/maxCount, i*255/maxCount, 0)
  fig1.line(x, y1-i*deltaY,line_width = 2, line_color = rgb1)
  fig1.line(x, y2-i*deltaY,line_width = 2, line_color = rgb2)

for i in range(0,maxCount):
  rgb1 = colors.RGB(0, 0, i*255/maxCount)
  rgb2 = colors.RGB(0, i*255/maxCount, 0)
  fig1.line(x, y1+i*deltaY,line_width = 2, line_color = rgb1)
  fig1.line(x, y2+i*deltaY,line_width = 2, line_color = rgb2)
  if (i % band_width == 0):
    fig1.line(x, y1+i*deltaY,line_width = 5, line_color =
white)

show(fig1)
```

Listing 4.11 starts with a commented out `pip3` code snippet that you can launch from the command line in order to install `Bokeh` (in case you haven't done so already).

The next code block contains several `Bokeh` -related statements as well as `NumPy` and `Math`.

Notice that the variable `white` is defined as an (R,G,B) triple of integers, which represents the red, green, and blue components of a color. In particular, (255,255,255) represents the color white (check online if you are unfamiliar with RGB). The next portion of Listing 4.11 initializes some scalar variables that are used in the two `for` loops that are in the second half of Listing 4.11.

Next, the `NumPy` variable `x` is a range of values from 0 to `math.PI/3`, with an increment of 0.05 between successive values. Then the `NumPy` variables `y1` and `y2` are defined as the sine and cosine values, respectively, of the values in `x`. The next code snippet initializes the variable `fig1` that represents a context in which the graphics effects will be rendered. This completes the initialization of the variables that are used in the two `for` loops.

The next portion of Listing 4.11 contains the first `for` loop that creates a gradient-like effect by defining (R,G,B) triples whose values are based partially on the value of the loop variable `i`. For example, the variable `rgb1` ranges in a linear fashion from (0,0,0) to (255,0,0), which represent the colors black and red, respectively. The variable `rgb2` ranges in a linear fashion from (0,0,0) to (255,255,0), which represent the colors black and yellow, respectively. The next portion of the `for` loop contains two invocations of the `fig1.line()` API that renders a sine wave and a cosine wave in the context variable `fig1`.

The second `for` loop is similar to the first `for` loop: the main difference is that the variable `rgb1` varies from black to blue, and the variable `rgb2` variables from black to green. The final code snippet in Listing 4.13 invokes the `show()` method that generates an `HTML` Web page (with the same prefix as the `Python` file) and then launches the Web page in a browser.

Figure 4.8 displays the graphics effect based on the code in Listing 4.11. If this image is displayed as black and white, launch the code from the command line and you will see the gradient-like effects in the image.

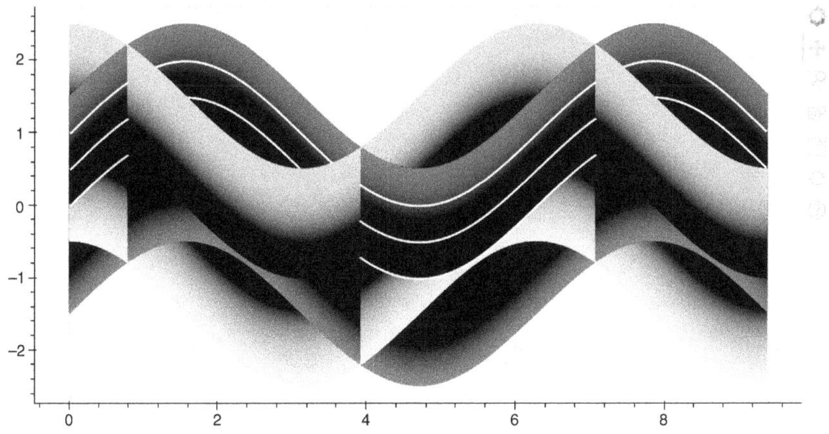

FIGURE 4.8 A Bokeh graphics sample.

The next section introduces you to `Scikit-learn`, which is a powerful `Python`-based library that supports many algorithms for machine learning. After you have read the short introduction, subsequent sections contain `Python` code samples that combine `Pandas`, `Matplotlib`, and `Scikit-learn` built-in datasets.

INTRODUCTION TO SCIKIT-LEARN

Since this book is about data visualization, you might be wondering why this chapter contains an introduction to `Scikit-learn` (also known as `Sklearn`). The reason is straightforward: the easy introduction to some `Scikit-learn` functionality is possible without a more formal learning process. In addition, this knowledge will bode well if you decide to delve into machine learning (and perhaps this section will provide additional motivation to do so).

However, a thorough understanding of `Scikit-learn` involves significantly more time and effort, especially if you plan to learn the details of the `Scikit-learn` machine learning algorithms. On the other hand, if you are not interested in learning about `Scikit-learn` at this point in time, you can skip this section and perhaps return to it when you are interested in learning this material.

`Scikit-learn` is Python's premier general-purpose machine learning library, and its home page is here:

https://scikit-learn.org/stable/

Before we discuss any code samples, please keep in mind that `Scikit-learn` is an immensely useful Python library that supports a huge number of machine learning algorithms. In particular, `Scikit-learn` supports many classification algorithms, such as logistic regression, naive Bayes, decision trees, random forests, and SVMs (support vector machines). Although entire books are available that are dedicated to `Scikit-learn`, this chapter contains only a few pages of Scikit-learn material.

If you decide that you want to acquire a deep level of knowledge about `Scikit-learn`, navigate to the Web pages that contain very detailed documentation for `Scikit-learn`. Moreover, if you have "how to" questions involving `Scikit-learn`, you can almost always find suitable answers on stack overflow (*https://stackoverflow.com/*).

`Scikit-learn` is well-suited for classification tasks as well as regression and clustering tasks in machine learning. `Scikit-learn` supports a vast collection of ML algorithms, including linear regression, logistic regression, kNN ("K nearest neighbor"), kMeans, decision trees, random forests, MLPs (multi-layer perceptrons), and SVMs (support vector machines).

Moreover, `Scikit-learn` supports dimensionality reduction techniques such as PCA (principal component analysis), "hyper parameter" tuning, methods for scaling data, and is suitable for preprocessing data, cross-validation, and so forth.

Machine learning code samples often contain a combination of `Scikit-learn`, NumPy, Pandas, and Matplotlib. In addition, `Scikit-learn` provides various built-in datasets that we can display visually. One of those datasets is the `Digits` dataset, which is the topic of the next section.

The next section of this chapter provides several Python code samples that contain a combination of Pandas, Matplotlib, and the Scikit-learn built-in Digits dataset.

THE DIGITS DATASET IN `Scikit-learn`

The `Digits` dataset in `Scikit-learn` comprises 1797 small 8x8 images: each image is a hand-written digit, which is also the case for the `MNIST` dataset. Listing 4.12 displays the contents of `load_digits1.py` that illustrates how to plot one of the digits in the `Digits` dataset.

LISTING 4.12: load_digits1.py

```
from scikit-learn import datasets

# Load in the 'digits' data
digits = datasets.load_digits()

# Print the 'digits' data
print(digits)
```

Listing 4.12 is very straightforward: after importing the `datasets` module, the variable `digits` is initialized with the contents of the `Digits` dataset. The `print()` statement displays the contents of the `digits` variable, which is displayed here:

```
{images': array(
     [[[0.,    0.,    5., ...,        1.,     0.,    0.],
       [0.,    0., 13., ...,  15.,    5.,     0.],
       [0.,    3., 15., ...,  11.,    8.,     0.],
       ...,
       [0.,    4., 11., ...,  12.,    7.,     0.],
       [0.,    2., 14., ...,  12.,    0.,     0.],
       [0.,    0.,    4., ...,    0.,    0.,     0.]]),
'target': array([0, 1, 2, ..., 8, 9, 8]), 'frame': None,
'feature_names': ['pixel_0_0', 'pixel_0_1', 'pixel_0_2', 'pixel_0_3',
'pixel_0_4', 'pixel_0_5', 'pixel_0_6', 'pixel_0_7', 'pixel_1_0',
'pixel_1_1', 'pixel_1_2', 'pixel_1_3', 'pixel_1_4', 'pixel_1_5',
'pixel_1_6', 'pixel_1_7', 'pixel_2_0', 'pixel_2_1', 'pixel_2_2',
'pixel_2_3', 'pixel_2_4', 'pixel_2_5', 'pixel_2_6', 'pixel_2_7',
'pixel_3_0', 'pixel_3_1', 'pixel_3_2', 'pixel_3_3', 'pixel_3_4',
'pixel_3_5', 'pixel_3_6', 'pixel_3_7', 'pixel_4_0', 'pixel_4_1',
'pixel_4_2', 'pixel_4_3', 'pixel_4_4', 'pixel_4_5', 'pixel_4_6',
'pixel_4_7', 'pixel_5_0', 'pixel_5_1', 'pixel_5_2', 'pixel_5_3',
'pixel_5_4', 'pixel_5_5', 'pixel_5_6', 'pixel_5_7', 'pixel_6_0',
'pixel_6_1', 'pixel_6_2', 'pixel_6_3', 'pixel_6_4', 'pixel_6_5',
'pixel_6_6', 'pixel_6_7', 'pixel_7_0', 'pixel_7_1', 'pixel_7_2',
'pixel_7_3', 'pixel_7_4', 'pixel_7_5', 'pixel_7_6', 'pixel_7_7'],
'target_names': array([0, 1, 2, 3, 4, 5, 6, 7, 8, 9]), 'images':
array([[[ 0.,  0.,  5., ...,  1.,  0.,  0.],
        [ 0.,  0., 13., ..., 15.,  5.,  0.],
        [ 0.,  3., 15., ..., 11.,  8.,  0.],
// data omitted for brevity
])}
```

Listing 4.13 displays the contents of `load_digits2.py` that illustrates how to plot one of the digits in the `Digits` dataset (which you can change in order to display a different digit).

LISTING 4.13: load_digits2.py

```
from sklearn.datasets import load_digits
from matplotlib import pyplot as plt

digits = load_digits()
#set interpolation='none'
```

```
fig = plt.figure(figsize=(3, 3))
plt.imshow(digits['images'][66], cmap="gray",
interpolation='none')
plt.show()
```

Listing 4.13 imports the `load_digits` class from `Scikit-learn` in order to initialize the variable `digits` with the contents of the `Digits` dataset that is available in `Scikit-learn`. The next portion of Listing 4.13 initializes the variable `fig` and invokes the method `imshow()` of the `plt` class in order to display a number in the `Digits` dataset.

Figure 4.9 displays a plot of one of the digits in the `Digits` dataset based on the code in Listing 4.13.

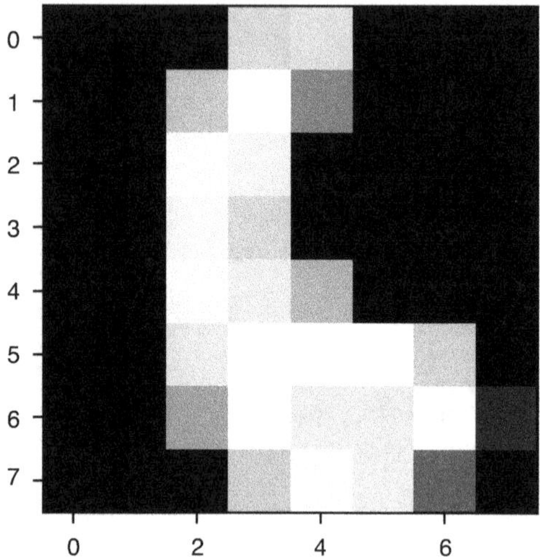

FIGURE 4.9 A digit in the Scikit-learn Digits dataset.

Listing 4.14 displays the contents of `load_digits3.py` that illustrates how to access the `Digits` dataset in `Scikit-learn`.

LISTING 4.14: load_digits3.py

```
from sklearn import datasets

digits = datasets.load_digits()
print("digits shape:",digits.images.shape)
print("data   shape:",digits.data.shape)

n_samples, n_features = digits.data.shape
print("(samples,features):", (n_samples, n_features))

import matplotlib.pyplot as plt
#plt.imshow(digits.images[-1], cmap=plt.cm.gray_r)
#plt.show()
```

```
plt.imshow(digits.images[0], cmap=plt.cm.binary,
interpolation='nearest')
plt.show()
```

Listing 4.14 starts with one `import` statement followed by the variable `digits that` contains the `Digits` dataset. The output from Listing 4.16 is here:

```
digits shape: (1797, 8, 8)
data   shape: (1797, 64)
(samples,features): (1797, 64)
```

Figure 4.10 displays an image in the `Digits` dataset based on the code in Listing 4.14.

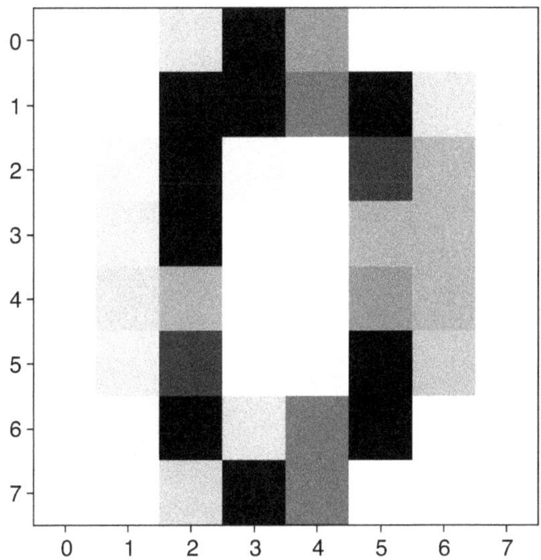

FIGURE 4.10 The digits in the Digits Dataset.

THE IRIS DATASET IN SCIKIT-LEARN

Listing 4.15 displays the contents of `sklearn_iris.py` that illustrates how to access the `Iris` dataset in `Scikit-learn`.

In addition to support for machine learning algorithms, `Scikit-learn` provides various built-in datasets that you can access with literally one line of code. In fact, Listing 4.15 displays the contents of `sklearn_iris1.py` that illustrates how you can easily load the `Iris` dataset into a `Pandas` DataFrame.

LISTING 4.15: sklearn_iris.py

```
import numpy as np
import pandas as pd
from scikit-learn.datasets import load_iris
```

```
iris = load_iris()

print("=> iris keys:")
for key in iris.keys():
  print(key)
print()

#print("iris dimensions:")
#print(iris.shape)
#print()

print("=> iris feature names:")
for feature in iris.feature_names:
  print(feature)
print()

X = iris.data[:, [2, 3]]
y = iris.target
print('=> Class labels:', np.unique(y))
print()

x_min, x_max = X[:, 0].min() - .5, X[:, 0].max() + .5
y_min, y_max = X[:, 1].min() - .5, X[:, 1].max() + .5

print("=> target:")
print(iris.target)
print()

print("=> all data:")
print(iris.data)
```

Listing 4.15 contains several import statements and then initializes the variable `iris` with the Iris dataset. Next, a `for` loop displays the keys in dataset, followed by another `for` loop that displays the feature names.

The next portion of Listing 4.15 initializes the variable `X` with the feature values in columns 2 and 3, and then initializes the variable `y` with the values of the target column.

The variable `x_min` is initialized as the minimum value of column 0 and then an additional 0.5 is subtracted from x_min. Similarly, the variable `x_max` is initialized as the maximum value of column 0 and then an additional 0.5 is added to `x_max`. The variables `y_min` and `y_max` are the counterparts to `x_min` and `x_max`, applied to column 1 instead of column 0.

Launch the code in Listing 4.15 and you will see the following output (truncated to save space):

```
Pandas df1:

=> iris keys:
data
target
target_names
```

```
DESCR
feature_names
filename

=> iris feature names:
sepal length (cm)
sepal width (cm)
petal length (cm)
petal width (cm)

=> Class labels: [0 1 2]

=> x_min: 0.5 x_max: 7.4
=> y_min: -0.4 y_max: 3.0

=> target:
[0 0 0 0 0 0 0 0 0 0 0 0 0 0 0 0 0 0 0 0 0 0 0 0 0 0 0 0 0 0 0 0 0 0 0 0 0
 0 0 0 0 0 0 0 0 0 0 0 0 0 1 1 1 1 1 1 1 1 1 1 1 1 1 1 1 1 1 1 1 1 1 1 1 1
 1 1 1 1 1 1 1 1 1 1 1 1 1 1 1 1 1 1 1 1 1 1 1 1 1 2 2 2 2 2 2 2 2 2 2 2 2
 2 2 2 2 2 2 2 2 2 2 2 2 2 2 2 2 2 2 2 2 2 2 2 2 2 2 2 2 2 2 2 2 2 2 2 2 2
 2 2]

=> all data:
[[5.1 3.5 1.4 0.2]
 [4.9 3.  1.4 0.2]
 [4.7 3.2 1.3 0.2]
 // details omitted for brevity
 [6.5 3.  5.2 2. ]
 [6.2 3.4 5.4 2.3]
 [5.9 3.  5.1 1.8]]
```

Scikit-Learn, Pandas, and the Iris Dataset

Listing 4.16 displays the contents of `pandas_iris.py` that illustrates how to load the contents of the `Iris` dataset (from Scikit-learn) into a `Pandas` DataFrame.

LISTING 4.16: pandas_iris.py

```
import numpy as np
import pandas as pd
from sklearn.datasets import load_iris

iris = load_iris()

print("=> IRIS feature names:")
for feature in iris.feature_names:
  print(feature)
print()

# Create a data frame with the feature variables
df = pd.Data frame(iris.data, columns=iris.feature_names)

print("=> number of rows:")
```

```
print(len(df))
print()

print("=> number of columns:")
print(len(df.columns))
print()

print("=> number of rows and columns:")
print(df.shape)
print()

print("=> number of elements:")
print(df.size)
print()

print("=> IRIS details:")
print(df.info())
print()

print("=> top five rows:")
print(df.head())
print()

X = iris.data[:, [2, 3]]
y = iris.target
print('=> Class labels:', np.unique(y))
```

Listing 4.16 contains several `import` statements and then initializes the variable `iris` with the Iris dataset. Next, a `for` loop displays the feature names. The next code snippet initializes the variable `df` as a `Pandas` DataFrame that contains the data from the `Iris` dataset.

The next block of code invokes some attributes and methods of a `Pandas` DataFrame to display the number of row, columns, and elements in the data frame, as well as the details of the `Iris` dataset, the first five rows, and the unique labels in the `Iris` dataset. Launch the code in Listing 4.16 and you will see the following output:

```
=> IRIS feature names:
sepal length (cm)
sepal width (cm)
petal length (cm)
petal width (cm)

=> number of rows:
150

=> number of columns:
4

=> number of rows and columns:
(150, 4)
=> number of elements:
```

```
600

=> IRIS details:
<class 'pandas.core.frame.Data frame'>
RangeIndex: 150 entries, 0 to 149
Data columns (total 4 columns):
sepal length (cm)     150 non-null float64
sepal width (cm)      150 non-null float64
petal length (cm)     150 non-null float64
petal width (cm)      150 non-null float64
dtypes: float64(4)
memory usage: 4.8 KB
None

=> top five rows:
   sepal length (cm)  sepal width (cm)  petal length (cm)  petal width (cm)
0                5.1               3.5                1.4               0.2
1                4.9               3.0                1.4               0.2
2                4.7               3.2                1.3               0.2
3                4.6               3.1                1.5               0.2
4                5.0               3.6                1.4               0.2

=> Class labels: [0 1 2]
```

ADVANCED TOPICS IN SEABORN

Listing 4.17 displays the contents `sns_kde_plot1.py` that displays a kde plot.

LISTING 4.17: sns_kde_plot1.py

```
import numpy as np
import matplotlib.pyplot as plt
import seaborn as sns

np.random.seed(1)
numerical_1 = np.random.randn(400)

np.random.seed(2)
numerical_2 = np.random.randn(400)

fig, ax = plt.subplots(figsize=(6,6))

sns.kdeplot(x=numerical_1,
            y= numerical_2,
            ax=ax,
            shade=True,
            color="blue",
            bw=1)
plt.show()
```

Listing 4.17 contains several `import` statements and then initializes the variables `numerical_1` and `numerical_2` with a set of 400 randomly generated numbers. The next code snippet initializes the figure-related variables `fig` and `ax`.

The next code snippet invokes the `kdeplot()` method of `Seaborn` and uses the values in `numerical_1` and `numerical_2` as values for the horizontal and vertical axes, respectively. The final code snippet displays the chart that is generated by the `kdeplot()` method. Now launch the code in Listing 4.17 and you will see the generated chart.

Figure 4.11 displays a plot of the data in the `Titanic` dataset based on the code in Listing 4.17.

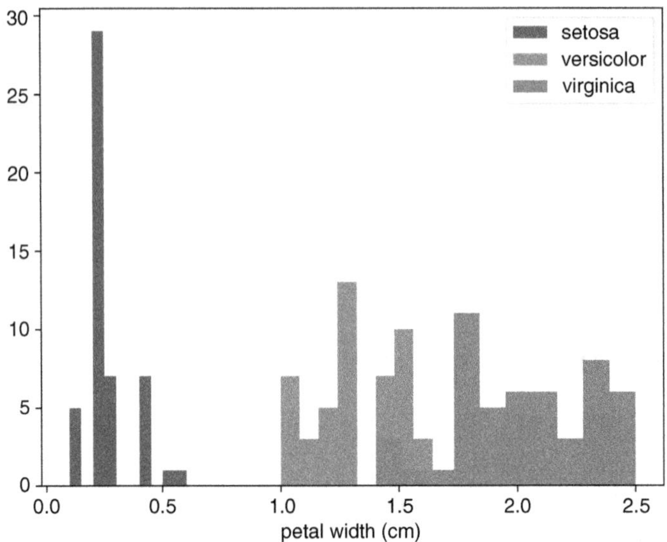

FIGURE 4.11 A Pandas DataFrame displayed via `Seaborn`.

Listing 4.18 displays the contents `sns_line_barchart1.py` that displays a line graph and a bar chart.

LISTING 4.18: sns_line_barchart1.py

```
import numpy as np

import seaborn as sns
import matplotlib.pyplot as plt

sns.set(style="white", rc={"lines.linewidth": 3})
fig, ax1 = plt.subplots(figsize=(4,4))
ax2 = ax1.twinx()
sns.barplot(x=['A','B','C','D'],
            y=[100,200,135,98],
            color='#004488',
            ax=ax1)

sns.lineplot(x=['A','B','C','D'],
             y=[4,2,5,3],
             color='r',
```

```
                marker="o",
                ax=ax2)

plt.show()
```

Listing 4.18 contains several `import` statements and then initializes the figure-related variables `fig` and `ax`, followed by the variable `ax2` that is initialized by invoking the `twinx()` method of `ax1`.

The next two code blocks generate a bar plot and a line plot, respectively, using hard-coded values for `x` and `y`. The next code snippet displays the generated bar chart and line plot. Figure 4.12 displays a bar chart and a line plot of the data in Listing 4.18.

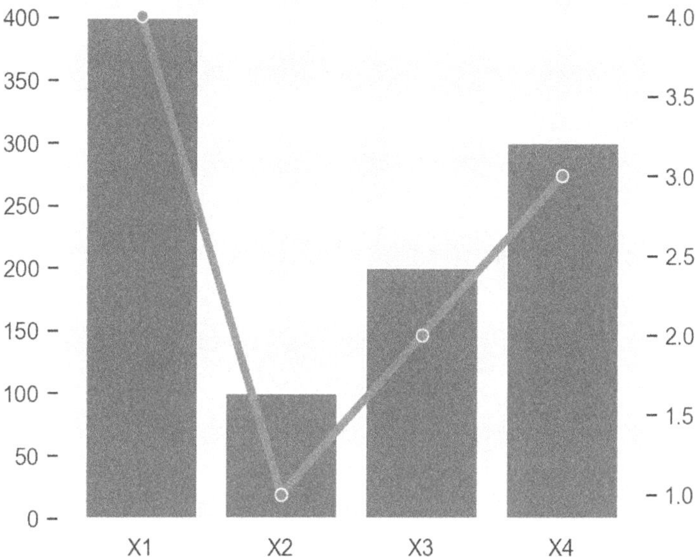

FIGURE 4.12 A bar chart and line graph.

SUMMARY

This chapter started with some basic features of `Seaborn`, which is an extension of `Matplotlib`. You saw examples of plotting lines and histograms, and also how to plot a `Pandas` DataFrame using `Seaborn`.

Next, you learned about `Bokeh`, along with an example of rendering graphics in `Bokeh`. Furthermore, you learned about `SVG` and how to render various 2D shapes, such as line segments, rectangles, circles, Bezier curves, and bar charts.

You also learned about `Scikit-learn`, including examples of working with the `Digits` and `Iris` datasets, and also how to process images. Finally, you learned how to render a bar chart and a line graph in `Scikit-learn`.

CHAPTER 5

GENERATIVE AI, BARD, AND GEMINI

This chapter contains information (some of which is AI-generated) about the main features of Bard, as well as some of its competitors. Please note that Bard has been renamed Gemini Pro as this book goes to print.

The first portion of this chapter starts with information (generated by Bard) regarding the nature of generative AI and conversational AI versus generative AI. According to Bard, it is true that Bard itself is included in generative AI.

The second portion of this chapter provides an overview of Gemini, followed by an introduction to Bard and some of its features, as well as some alternatives to Bard.

WHAT IS GENERATIVE AI?

Generative AI refers to a subset of artificial intelligence models and techniques that are designed to generate new data samples that are similar in nature to a given set of input data. The goal is to produce content or data that was not part of the original training set, but is coherent, contextually relevant, and in the same style or structure.

Generative AI is arguably unique in its ability to create and innovate with information, as opposed to merely analyzing or classifying it. The advancements in this field have led to breakthroughs in creative domains and practical applications, making it a cutting-edge area of AI research and development.

Key Features of Generative AI

The following list contains key features of generative AI, followed by a brief description for each item:

- Data generation
- Synthesis
- Learning distributions

Data generation refers to the ability to create new data points that are not part of the training data but resemble it. This can include text, images, music, videos, or any other form of data.

Synthesis means that generative models can blend various inputs to generate outputs that incorporate features from each input, like merging the styles of two images.

Learning distributions means that generative AI models learn the probability distribution of the training data so they can produce new samples from that distribution.

Popular Techniques in Generative AI

Generative Adversarial Networks (GANs): GANs consist of two networks, a generator and a discriminator, that are trained simultaneously. The generator tries to produce fake data, while the discriminator tries to distinguish between real data and fake data. Over time, the generator gets better at producing realistic data.

Variational Autoencoders (VAEs): VAEs are probabilistic models that learn to encode and decode data in a manner so that the encoded representations can be used to generate new data samples.

Recurrent Neural Networks (RNNs): Used primarily for sequence generation, such as text or music.

What Makes Generative AI Unique

Creation vs. Classification: While most traditional AI models aim to classify input data into predefined categories, generative models aim to create new data.

Unsupervised Learning: Many generative models, especially GANs and VAEs, operate in an unsupervised manner, meaning they do not require labeled data for training.

Diverse Outputs: Generative models can produce a wide variety of outputs based on learned distributions, making them ideal for tasks like art generation, style transfer, and more.

Challenges: Generative AI poses unique challenges, such as mode collapse in GANs or ensuring the coherence of generated content.

Furthermore, there are numerous areas that involve generative AI applications, some of which are listed in the following list:

- Art and music creation
- Data augmentation
- Style transfer
- Text generation
- Image synthesis
- Drug discovery

Art and music creation includes generating paintings, music, or other forms of art.

Data augmentation involves creating additional data for training models, especially when the original dataset is limited.

Style transfer refers to applying the style of one image to the content of another.

Text generation is a popular application of generative AI that involves creating coherent and contextually relevant text.

Image synthesis is another popular area of generative AI, and it involves generating realistic images, faces, or even creating scenes for video games.

Drug discovery is an important facet of generative AI that pertains to generating molecular structures for new potential drugs.

CONVERSATIONAL AI VERSUS GENERATIVE AI

Both conversational AI and generative AI are prominent subfields within the broader domain of artificial intelligence. However, these subfields have a different focus regarding their primary objective, the technologies that they use, and applications. Please read the following article for more information:

https://medium.com/@social_65128/differences-between-conversational-ai-and-generative-ai-e3adca2a8e9a

The primary differences between the two subfields are in the following sequence of points:

- Primary objective
- Applications
- Technologies used
- Training and Interaction
- Evaluation
- Data requirements

Primary Objective

The main goal of conversational AI is to facilitate human-like interactions between machines and humans. This includes chatbots, virtual assistants, and other systems that engage in dialogues with users.

The primary objective of generative AI is to create new content or data that was not in the training set but is not necessarily similar in structure and style to the original data. This can range from generating images, music, and text to more complex tasks like video synthesis.

Applications

Common applications for conversational AI include customer support chatbots, voice-operated virtual assistants (like Siri or Alexa), and interactive voice response (IVR) systems.

There is a broad spectrum of common applications for generative AI, such as creating art or music, generating realistic video game environments, synthesizing voices, and producing realistic images or even deep fakes.

Technologies Used

Conversational AI often relies on Natural Language Processing (NLP) techniques to understand and generate human language. This includes intent recognition, entity extraction, and dialogue management.

Generative AI commonly utilizes Generative Adversarial Networks (GANs), Variational Autoencoders (VAEs), and other generative models to produce new content.

Training and Interaction

While training can be supervised, semi-supervised, or unsupervised, the primary interaction mode for conversational AI is through back-and-forth dialogue or conversation.

The training process for generative AI, especially with models like GANs, involves iterative processes where the model learns to generate data by trying to fool a discriminator into believing the generated data is real.

Evaluation

Conversational AI evaluation metrics often revolve around understanding and response accuracy, user satisfaction, and the fluency of generated responses.

Generative AI evaluation metrics for models like GANs can be challenging and might involve using a combination of quantitative metrics and human judgment to assess the quality of generated content.

Data Requirements

Data requirements for conversational AI typically involve dialogue data from conversations between humans or between humans and bots.

Data requirements for generative AI involve large datasets of the kind of content it is supposed to generate, such as images, text, or music.

Although both conversational AI and generative AI deal with generating outputs, their primary objectives, applications, and methodologies can differ significantly. Conversational AI is used for interactive communication with users, while generative AI focuses on producing new, original content.

IS GEMINI PART OF GENERATIVE AI?

Gemini is an LLM that is considered an example of generative AI. Bard belongs to a class of models called "transformers," which are particularly adept at handling sequences of data, such as text-related tasks.

The following list provides various reasons why Gemini is considered generative, followed by a brief description of each item:

- Text generation
- Learning distributions
- Broad applications
- Unsupervised learning

Text Generation: These models can produce coherent, contextually relevant, and often highly sophisticated sequences of text based on given prompts. They generate responses that were not explicitly present in their training data but are constructed based on the patterns and structures they learned during training.

Learning Distributions: Gemini (as well as GPT-3, GPT-4, and similar models) learn the probability distribution of their training data. When generating text, they are essentially sampling from this learned distribution to produce sequences that are likely based on their training.

Broad Applications: Beyond just text-based chat or conversation, these models can be used for a variety of generative tasks like story writing, code generation, poetry, and even creating content in specific styles or mimicking certain authors, showcasing their generative capabilities.

Unsupervised Learning: While they can be fine-tuned with specific datasets, models like GPT-3 are primarily trained in an unsupervised manner on vast amounts of text, learning to generate content without requiring explicit labeled data for every possible response.

In essence, Google Gemini is a quintessential example of generative AI in the realm of NLP and generation.

The next several sections briefly introduce some of the AI companies that have a strong presence in the market.

DEEPMIND

DeepMind has made significant contributions to AI, which includes the creation of various AI systems. DeepMind was established in 2010 and became a subsidiary of Google 2014, and its home page is at *https://deepmind.com/*.

DeepMind created the 280 GB language model Gopher, which significantly outperformed its competitors, including GPT-3, J1-Jumbo, and MT-NLG. DeepMind also developed AlphaFold, which solved a protein folding task that had eluded researchers for ten years in only 30 minutes. Moreover, DeepMind made AlphaFold available for free for everyone in July 2021. DeepMind has made significant contributions in the development of AI game systems, some of which are discussed in the next section.

DeepMind and Games

DeepMind powers the AI systems AlphaStar, which plays StarCraft, and AlphaGo, which defeated the best human players in Go (the game is considerably more difficult than chess). These games provide "perfect information," whereas games with "imperfect information" (such as poker) have posed challenges for ML models.

AlphaGo Zero (the successor of AlphaGo) mastered the game through self-play in less time and with less computing power than AlphaGo. AlphaGo Zero exhibited extraordinary performance by defeating AlphaGo 100 - 0. Another powerful system is AlphaZero, which used a self-play technique to learn to play Go, chess, and shogi, and also achieved SOTA (State Of The Art) performance results.

By way of comparison, ML models that use tree search are well-suited for games with perfect information. Games with imperfect information (such as poker) involve hidden information that can be leveraged to devise counter strategies to counteract the strategies of opponents. In particular, AlphaStar is capable of playing against the best players of StarCraft II, and became the first AI to achieve SOTA results in a game that requires a highly strategic methodology.

Player of Games (PoG)

The DeepMind team at Google devised the general-purpose PoG (Player of Games) algorithm that is based on the following techniques:

- CFR (counterfactual regret minimization)
- CVPN (counterfactual value-and-policy network)
- GT-CFT (growing tree CFR)
- CVPN

The counterfactual value-and-policy network (CVPN) is a neural network that calculates the counterfactuals for each state belief in the game. This is important for evaluating the different variants of the game at any given time.

Growing tree CFR (GT-CFR) is a variation of CFR that is optimized for game-trees trees that grow over time. GT-CFR is based on two fundamental phases, which is discussed in more detail online:

https://medium.com/syncedreview/deepminds-pog-excels-in-perfect-and-imperfect-information-games-advancing-research-on-general-9dbad5c04221

OPENAI

OpenAI is an AI research company that has made significant contributions to AI, including DALL-E and Bard, and its home page is at *https://openai.com/api/*.

OpenAI was founded in San Francisco by Elon Musk and Sam Altman (as well as others), and one of its stated goals is to develop AI that benefits humanity. Given Microsoft's massive investments in and deep alliance with the organization, OpenAI might be viewed as an arm of Microsoft. OpenAI is the creator of the GPT-x series of LLMs (Large Language Models), as well as Bard, which was made available on November 30, 2022.

In addition, OpenAI developed DALL-E, which generates images from text. OpenAI initially did not permit users to upload images that contained realistic faces. Later (in the fourth quarter of 2022), OpenAI changed its policy to allow users to upload faces into its online system. Check the OpenAI Web page for more details.

OpenAI has also released a public beta of Embeddings, which is a data format that is suitable for various types of tasks with machine learning, as described here:

https://beta.openai.com/docs/guides/embeddings

OpenAI is the creator of Codex, which provides a set of models that were trained using NLP. The initial release of Codex was in private beta, and more information is accessible at *https://beta.openai.com/docs/engines/instruct-series-beta*.

OpenAI offers four models that are collectively called their "Instruct" models, which support the ability of GPT-3 to generate natural language. These models will be deprecated in early January 2024 and replaced with updated versions of GPT-3, Bard, and GPT-4.

If you want to learn more about the features and services that OpenAI offers, navigate to the following website: *https://platform.openai.com/overview*.

COHERE

Cohere is a start-up and a competitor of OpenAI, and its home page is at *https://cohere.ai/*.

Cohere develops cutting-edge NLP technology that is commercially available for multiple industries. Cohere is focused on models that perform textual analysis instead of models for text generation (such as GPT-based models). The founding team of Cohere is impressive: CEO Aidan Gomez is one of the co-inventors of the transformer architecture, and CTO Nick Frost is a protege of Geoff Hinton.

HUGGING FACE

Hugging Face is a popular community-based repository for open-source NLP technology, and its home page is at *https://github.com/huggingface*.

Unlike OpenAI or Cohere, Hugging Face does not build its own NLP models. Instead, Hugging Face is a platform that manages a plethora of open-source NLP models that customers can fine-tune and then deploy those fine-tuned models. Indeed, Hugging Face has become the eminent location for people to collaborate on NLP models because of the plethora of LLMs that it makes available to users.

Hugging Face Libraries

Hugging Face offers three important libraries: datasets, tokenizers, and transformers. The Accelerate library supports PyTorch models. The datasets library provides an assortment of libraries for NLP. The tokenizers library enables you to convert text data to numeric values.

Perhaps the most impressive library is the transformers library, which provides an enormous set of pre-trained BERT-based models that can perform a wide variety of NLP tasks. The Github repository is available at *https://github.com/huggingface/transformers*.

Hugging Face Model Hub

Hugging Face provides a model hub that offers a plethora of models that are accessible online. Moreover, the website supports online testing of its models, which includes the following tasks:

- Masked word completion with BERT
- Name Entity Recognition with Electra
- Natural Language Inference with RoBERTa
- Question answering with DistilBERT
- Summarization with BART
- Text generation with GPT-2
- Translation with T5

Navigate to the following website and follow the guidelines in order to see the text generation capabilities of "writing with a transformer:" *https://transformer.huggingface.co*.

In a subsequent chapter, you will see Python code samples that show how to list all the available Hugging Face datasets as well as how to load a specific dataset.

AI21

AI21 is a company that provides proprietary large language models via API to support the applications of its customers. The current SOTA model of AI21 is called Jurassic-1 (roughly the same size as GPT-3), and AI21 also creates its own applications on top of Jurassic-1 and other models. The current application suite of AI21 involves tools that can augment reading and writing.

Primer is an older competitor in this space, founded two years before the invention of the transformer. The company primarily serves clients in government and defense.

INFLECTIONAI

A newer AI company is InflectionAI, whose highly impressive founding team includes:

- Reid Hoffman (LinkedIn)
- DeepMind cofounder Mustafa Suleyman
- DeepMind researcher Karen Simonyan

InflectionAI is committed to a challenging task: enabling humans to interact with computers in much the same way that humans communicate with each other.

ANTHROPIC

Anthropic was created in 2021 by former employees of OpenAI, and its home page is at *https://www.anthropic.com/*.

Anthropic has significant financial support from an assortment of companies, including Google and Salesforce. As this book goes to print, Anthropic released Claude 2 as a competitor to Bard.

Claude 2 has the ability to summarize as much as 75,000 words of text-based content, whereas Bard currently has a limit of 3,000 words. Moreover, Claude 2 achieved a score of 76.5% on portions of the bar exam and 71% in a Python coding test. Claude 2 also has a higher rate than Bard in terms of providing "clean" responses to queries from users.

This concludes the portion of the chapter regarding the AI companies that are making important contributions in AI. The next section provides a high-level introduction to LLMs (large language models).

WHAT IS PROMPT ENGINEERING?

Prompt engineering refers to devising text-based prompts that enable AI-based systems to improve the output that is generated, which means that the output more closely matches whatever users want to produce from AI-systems. By way of analogy, think of prompts as similar to the role of coaches: they offer advice and suggestions to help people perform better in their given tasks.

Since prompts are based on words, the challenge involves learning how different words can affect the generated output. Moreover, it is difficult to predict how systems respond to a given prompt. For instance, if you want to generate a landscape, the difference between a dark landscape and a bright landscape is intuitive. However, if you want a beautiful landscape, how would an AI system generate a corresponding image? As you can surmise, concrete words are easier than abstract or subjective words for AI systems that generate images from text. Just to add more detail to the previous example, how would you visualize the following images?

- A beautiful landscape
- A beautiful song
- A beautiful movie

Although prompt engineering started with text-to-image generation, there are other types of prompt engineering, such as audio-based prompts, that interpret emphasized text and emotions that are detected in speech, and sketch-based prompts that generate images from drawings. The most recent focus of attention involves text-based prompts for generating videos, which presents exciting opportunities for artists and designers. An example of image-to-image processing is accessible online at the following site:

https://huggingface.co/spaces/fffiloni/stable-diffusion-color-sketch

Prompts and Completions

A *prompt* is a text string that users provide to LLMs, and a *completion* is the text that users receive from LLMs. Prompts assist LLMs in completing a request (task), and they can vary in length. Although prompts can be any text string, including a random string, the quality and structure of prompts affects the quality of completions.

Think of prompts as a mechanism for giving "guidance" to LLMs or even as a way to "coach" LLMs into providing desired answers. Keep in mind that the number of tokens in a prompt plus the number of tokens in the completion can be at most 2,048 tokens.

Types of Prompts

The following list contains well-known types prompts for LLMs:

- zero-shot prompts
- one-shot prompts
- few-shot prompts
- instruction prompts

A *zero-shot prompt* contains a description of a task, whereas a *one-shot prompt* consists of a single example for completing a task. As you can probably surmise, *few-shot prompts* consist of multiple examples (typically between 10 and 100). In all cases, a clear description of the task or tasks is recommended: more tasks provide GPT-3 with more information, which in turn can lead to more accurate completions.

T0 (for "zero shot") is an interesting LLM: although T0 is 16 times smaller (11 GB) than GPT-3 (175 GB), T0 has outperformed GPT-3 on language-related tasks. T0 can perform well on unseen NLP tasks (i.e., tasks that are new to T0) because it was trained on a dataset containing multiple tasks.

The following set of links provide the Github repository for T0, a Web page for training T0 directly in a browser, and a 3 GB version of T0, respectively:

https://github.com/bigscience-workshop/t-zero

As you can probably surmise, T0++ is based on T0, and it was trained with extra tasks beyond the set of tasks on which T0 was trained.

Here is another detail to keep in mind: the first three prompts in the preceding list are also called *zero-shot learning, one-shot learning*, and *few-shot learning*.

Instruction Prompts

Instruction prompts are used for fine tuning LLMs, and they specify a format (determined by you) for the manner in which the LLM is expected to conform in its responses. You can prepare your own instruction prompts or you can access prompt template libraries that contain different templates for different tasks, along with different data sets. Various prompt instruction templates are publicly available, such as the following links that provides prompt templates for Llama:

https://github.com/devbrones/llama-prompts

https://pub.towardsai.net/llama-gpt4all-simplified-local-Bard-ab7d28d34923

Reverse Prompts

Another technique uses a reverse order: input prompts are answers, and the responses are the questions associated with the answers (similar to a popular game show). For example, given a French sentence, you might ask the model, "What English text might have resulted in this French translation?"

System Prompts Versus Agent Prompts

The distinction between a system prompt and an agent prompt often comes up in the context of conversational AI systems and chatbot design.

A *system prompt* is typically an initial message or cue given by the system to guide the user on what they can do or to set expectations about the interaction. It often serves as an introduction or a way to guide users on how to proceed. Here are some examples of system prompts:

- `"Welcome to ChatBotX! You can ask me questions about weather, news, or sports. How can I assist you today?"`
- `"Hello! For account details, press 1. For technical support, press 2."`
- `"Greetings! Type 'order' to track your package or 'help' for assistance."`

By contrast, an *agent prompt* is a message generated by the AI model or agent in response to a user's input during the course of an interaction. It is a part of the back-and-forth exchange within the conversation. The agent prompt guides the user to provide more information, clarifies ambiguity, or nudges the user towards a specific action. Here are some examples of agent prompts:

- `User: "I'm looking for shoes."`
  `Agent Prompt: "Great! Are you looking for men's or women's shoes?"`
- `User: "I can't log in."`
  `Agent Prompt: "I'm sorry to hear that. Can you specify if you're having trouble with your password or username?"`
- `User: "Tell me a joke."`
  `Agent Prompt: "Why did the chicken join a band? Because it had the drumsticks!"`

The fundamental difference between the two is their purpose and placement in the interaction. A system prompt is often at the beginning of an interaction, setting the stage for the conversation. An agent prompt occurs during the conversation, steering the direction of the dialogue based on user input.

Both types of prompts are crucial for creating a fluid and intuitive conversational experience for users. They guide the user and help ensure that the system understands and addresses the user's needs effectively.

Prompt Templates

Prompt templates are predefined formats or structures used to instruct a model or system to perform a specific task. They serve as a foundation for generating prompts, where certain parts of the template can be filled in or customized to produce a variety of specific prompts. By way of analogy, prompt templates are the counterpart to macros that you can define in some text editors.

Prompt templates are especially useful when working with language models, as they provide a consistent way to query the model across multiple tasks or data points. In particular, prompt templates can make it easier to:

- ensure consistency when querying a model multiple times
- facilitate batch processing or automation
- reduce errors and variations in how questions are posed to the model

As an example, suppose you're working with an LLM and you want to translate English sentences into French. An associated prompt template could be the following:

"Translate the following English sentence into French: {sentence}"

Note that {sentence} is a placeholder that you can replace with any English sentence.

You can use the preceding prompt template to generate specific prompts:

- "Translate the following English sentence into French: 'Hello, how are you?'"
- "Translate the following English sentence into French: 'I love ice cream.'"

As you can see, prompt templates enable you to easily generate a variety of prompts for different sentences without having to rewrite the entire instruction each time. In fact, this concept can be extended to more complex tasks and can incorporate multiple placeholders or more intricate structures, depending on the application.

Poorly-Worded Prompts

When crafting prompts, it is crucial to be as clear and specific as possible to guide the response in the desired direction. Ambiguous or vague prompts can lead to a wide range of responses, many of which might not be useful or relevant to the user's actual intent.

Moreover, poorly-worded prompts are often vague, ambiguous, or too broad, and they can lead to confusion, misunderstanding, or non-specific responses from AI models. Here is a list of examples of poorly-worded prompts:

"Tell me about that thing."
Problem: Too vague. What "thing" is being referred to?

"Why did it happen?"
Problem: No context. What event or situation is being discussed?

"Explain stuff."
Problem: Too broad. What specific "stuff" should be explained?

"Do what is needful."
Problem: Ambiguous. What specific action is required?

"I want information."
Problem: Not specific. What type of information is desired?

"Can you get me the thing from the place?"
Problem: Both "thing" and "place" are unclear.

"Can you tell me about 'What's-his-name's' book?"
Problem: Ambiguous reference. Who is "his?"

"How do you do the process?"
Problem: Which "process" is being referred to?

"Describe the importance of the topic."
Problem: The "topic" is not specified.

"Why is it bad or good?"
Problem: No context. What is "it"?

"Help with the issue."
Problem: Vague. What specific issue is being faced?

"Things to consider for the task."
Problem: Ambiguous. What "task" is being discussed?

"How does this work?"
Problem: Lack of specificity. What is "this?"

WHAT IS GEMINI?

Gemini is the most advanced LLM from Google and is the foundation for Bard. Google plans to integrate Gemini into some of its other products, such as YouTube and Google Search.

Gemini is available in three sizes: *Nano* for mobile devices (such as Pixel 8), *Pro* for Bard, and *Ultra*, the most sophisticated of the three models (which was released in February/2024).

Gemini is a multimodal LLM that can process various types of input, including text, code, audio, images, and videos. Gemini generated some of the Python code samples in Chapters 3 and 4, as well as all the Python code samples in Chapter 6. However, some of the multimodal features of Gemini will become available at a later point in time. Gemini also sometimes suffers from so-called "hallucinations," which is common for LLMs.

Gemini Ultra Versus GPT-4

Google performed a comparison of Gemini Ultra and GPT-4 from OpenAI, and Ultra outperformed GPT-4 on seven of eight text-based tests. Moreover, Ultra outperformed GPT-4 on ten out of ten multimodal tests. In many cases, Ultra outperformed GPT-4 by a fairly small margin, which means that both LLMs are competitive in terms of functionality. Note that thus far Google has not provided a comparison of Gemini Pro or Gemini Nano with GPT-4.

Gemini Strengths

As you probably expected, Gemini has strengths and weaknesses, just like any other LLM. This section provides a brief description of the major strengths of Gemini.

1. *Accuracy and factuality*: Bard was trained on a massive dataset of text and code, including factual information from Google Search. This allows it to provide accurate and reliable answers to factual questions.
2. *Comprehensiveness*: Bard provides more comprehensive and detailed answers than other large language models. It retrieves relevant information from its database and presents it in a clear and concise manner.
3. *User-friendly interface*: Bard has a user-friendly interface that is easy to navigate and use. It allows users to edit their questions, upvote and downvote responses, and search for information on the Web.
4. *Multiple response formats*: Bard can generate text in various formats, including poems, code, scripts, musical pieces, emails, and letters. This makes it versatile and adaptable to different tasks.
5. *Free to use*: Bard is currently free to use, which makes it accessible to a wide audience.

Gemini's Weaknesses

The previous section discusses the strengths of Gemini, whereas this section provides a brief description of the major weaknesses of Gemini.

1. *Creativity*: While Bard can generate creative text formats, it sometimes lacks originality and can be repetitive. It struggles with tasks that require a high level of imagination and out-of-the-box thinking.
2. *Conversational flow*: Bard can be unnatural in conversations. Its responses may not always flow smoothly or follow the context of the conversation.
3. *Technical knowledge*: Although trained on a massive dataset, Bard can struggle with technical questions or tasks that require specialized knowledge in specific domains.
4. *Limited integrations*: Compared to ChatGPT, Bard has fewer integrations with other apps and services. This limits its functionality and flexibility.
5. *Limited customizability*: Users currently have limited options to customize Bard's behavior or preferences.

Gemini Nano on Mobile Devices

Gemini Nano has features such as grammar correction, proofreading, and text summarization. Moreover, a software update for the Android Pixel 8 Pro is available to provide access to Gemini Nano on mobile devices. Other features will be supported on mobile devices in the coming months.

Google has also created Android AICore, which is a system service that provides access to Nano on Android devices. This service supports improved safety and model management in a manner that makes it easier for you to incorporate AI into Android devices.

WHAT IS BARD?

Bard is a chatbot from Google that has been updated with Gemini Pro, which is one of the three Gemini LLMs that are available from Google. Navigate to the following URL to access Bard:

https://bard.google.com/chat/2d66dfbbf91ab734

Currently, Bard is not multimodal: it only supports text prompts. Moreover, Bard is only available in English, which will be expanded at a later date.

Gemini Pro is now available for cloud-based services, such as Google AI Studio as well as Google Cloud Vertex AI: navigate to their respective home pages for additional details. Google says it aims to add Gemini Ultra to Bard in 2024. It will be able to handle different modal types, from images to audio, and will "think more carefully before answering" tricky questions. This version will be called Bard Advanced.

Gemini Pro in Google Bard is free and does not require any payment or credit system to use. Likewise, the Gemini Nano came to the Pixel 8 Pro smartphone in a free update.

It is possible that Google will charge for Gemini Ultra given its more powerful capabilities, in a similar way to how OpenAI charges $20 a month for access to ChatGPT Plus. Thus far, there has been no official statement about this from Google: periodically check online for any updates from Google.

In terms of functionality, Bard can perform a multitude of tasks, some of which are listed below:

- write poetry
- write essays
- write code
- role play
- reject inappropriate requests

Bard also provides "prompt replies," which are examples of what you can ask Bard.

SAMPLE QUERIES AND RESPONSES FROM BARD

The following section has five examples of various queries submitted to Bard, followed by the detailed response from Bard.

EXAMPLE 1

User: Many people think that AI is dangerous. What do you think?

Bard: Whether AI is dangerous is a complex question with no easy answer. There are valid arguments on both sides of the debate.

Potential dangers of AI:

- **Job displacement:** As AI becomes more sophisticated, it has the potential to automate many tasks currently performed by humans, leading to widespread job losses. This could have significant social and economic consequences.
- **Bias and discrimination:** AI systems can inherit and amplify biases present in the data they are trained on. This could lead to discriminatory outcomes, particularly in areas like law enforcement, credit scoring, and hiring.
- **Autonomous weapons:** The development of autonomous weapons systems that can operate without human intervention raises ethical and security concerns. These weapons could be used for malicious purposes or malfunction with devastating consequences.
- **Loss of control:** As AI systems become more complex and powerful, it is possible that we may lose control over them. This could lead to unintended consequences or even catastrophic outcomes.

Benefits and potential for good of AI:

- **Solving global challenges:** AI can be used to address some of the world's most pressing challenges, such as climate change, poverty, and disease. By automating tasks and analyzing large datasets, AI can help us to find more efficient and effective solutions.
- **Improving healthcare:** AI has the potential to revolutionize healthcare by providing more accurate diagnoses, personalized treatments, and improved patient care. AI can also be used to develop new drugs and therapies.
- **Enhancing human capabilities:** AI can be used to augment human intelligence and capabilities in various areas, such as education, research, and creative endeavors. This can lead to breakthroughs and innovations that would not be possible without AI.
- **Economic prosperity:** AI can drive economic growth and create new industries and jobs. By automating tasks and improving efficiency, AI can help businesses to be more productive and competitive.

Ultimately, whether AI is dangerous or beneficial depends on how it is developed and used. It is important to ensure that AI is developed responsibly and ethically, with safeguards in place to mitigate potential risks. We must also be mindful of the potential benefits of AI and work to ensure that it is used for the betterment of humanity.

It is important to consider the various perspectives on this issue and to engage in open and informed discussion about the future of AI. By working together, we can ensure that AI is used for good and not for harm.

EXAMPLE 2

Here is another example of a query submitted to Bard, followed by its detailed response:

User: What are some ways in which you can improve the accuracy of your responses to queries?

Bard: There are several ways to improve the accuracy of my responses to queries:

Data:

- **Larger and more diverse datasets:** Training on larger and more diverse datasets exposes me to a wider variety of language and information, improving my ability to generalize and generate accurate responses.
- **Higher quality data:** Focusing on data that is accurate, consistent, and relevant to specific tasks can significantly enhance my performance.
- **Domain-specific data:** Fine-tuning my training on datasets related to specific domains allows me to become an expert in those areas and provide more accurate and relevant responses.

Model Architecture:

- **More complex models:** Utilizing more sophisticated neural network architectures with greater depth and capacity can enable me to learn more complex relationships and generate more accurate outputs.
- **Ensemble models:** Combining predictions from multiple models can help to reduce bias and improve overall accuracy.
- **Model regularization techniques:** Techniques like dropout and weight decay can prevent overfitting and improve the generalizability of the model.

Training and Optimization:

- **Transfer learning:** Leveraging knowledge gained from pre-trained models on large datasets can significantly accelerate my learning process and improve performance on new tasks.
- **Multi-task learning:** Training me on multiple related tasks simultaneously can help me to learn more generalizable representations and improve performance across all tasks.
- **Active learning:** Focusing on learning from the most informative examples can significantly improve the efficiency and accuracy of the training process.

Evaluation and Feedback:

- **Human evaluation:** Regularly evaluating my responses through human feedback allows me to identify areas for improvement and prioritize the development of new capabilities.
- **Error analysis:** Analyzing common errors I make helps me to understand the causes of those errors and develop strategies to avoid them in the future.
- **Explainability and interpretability:** Developing techniques to explain my reasoning and the rationale behind my responses can help me to build trust and gain user confidence in my accuracy.

By continuously incorporating these strategies and advancements in AI and language modeling, I can strive to provide increasingly accurate and informative responses to your queries.

EXAMPLE 3

User: Can you give an example of an odd perfect number?

Bard: Unfortunately, it is not known whether odd perfect numbers exist. While there are infinitely many even perfect numbers, the existence of odd perfect numbers remains a mathematical problem with no confirmed solution.

Despite extensive research, no odd perfect number has been found yet. Mathematicians have proven several key properties related to odd perfect numbers, which provide some clues about their potential existence:

- **Odd perfect numbers must be greater than 10^1500.** This means that if an odd perfect number exists, it must be a very large number.
- **Odd perfect numbers are not divisible by 105.** This eliminates a large number of potential candidates from the search.
- **Odd perfect numbers must have the form N ≡ 1 (mod 12) or N ≡ 117 (mod 468) or N ≡ 81 (mod 324).** These congruences provide further restrictions on the possible forms of an odd perfect number.

While these properties offer valuable information, they haven't led to a definitive answer about the existence of odd perfect numbers. The search for them continues to be an active area of research in mathematics.

If you're interested in learning more about this fascinating mathematical problem, I encourage you to explore additional resources on odd perfect numbers. Here are some links that might be helpful:

- **Wikipedia article on odd perfect numbers:** *https://en.wikipedia.org/wiki/Perfect_number*
- **MathWorld article on odd perfect numbers:** *https://reference.wolfram.com/language/ref/PerfectNumber.html*
- **Numberphile video on odd perfect numbers:** *https://m.youtube.com/watch?v=0p1QsPRJcAU*

I hope this information is helpful!

EXAMPLE 4

User: Can you provide a proof of Goldbach's conjecture? Bard: Unfortunately, I cannot provide a complete proof of Goldbach's Conjecture at this time. While significant progress has been made towards proving it, a full and definitive proof remains elusive.

However, I can offer some information about the conjecture itself and the progress made towards proving it:

Goldbach's Conjecture: Every even integer greater than 2 can be expressed as the sum of two prime numbers.

Progress towards a proof:

- **Weak Goldbach's Conjecture:** Every odd integer greater than 5 can be expressed as the sum of three prime numbers. This was proven by Harald Helfgott in 2013.

- **Vinogradov's Theorem:** This theorem, proven in 1937, provided significant insights into the distribution of prime numbers and paved the way for further advancements in understanding Goldbach's Conjecture.
- **Chen Jingrun's Theorem:** This theorem, proven in 1966, showed that every sufficiently large even number can be expressed as the sum of a prime and the product of two primes.
- **Improvements on Chen's Theorem:** Numerous refinements and improvements have been made on Chen's Theorem, pushing the lower bound for sufficiently large even numbers even further.

Despite these advancements, complete proof for Goldbach's Conjecture still remains an open problem in mathematics. The complexity of the conjecture and the vastness of the number system make it an extremely challenging problem to tackle.

Here are some resources where you can find more information about Goldbach's Conjecture and the progress towards a proof:

- **Wikipedia article on Goldbach's Conjecture:** *https://simple.wikipedia.org/wiki/Goldbach%27s_conjecture*
- **MathWorld article on Goldbach's Conjecture:** *https://resources.wolframcloud.com/FunctionRepository/resources/Goldbach/*
- **Numberphile video on Goldbach's Conjecture:** *https://m.youtube.com/watch?v=MxiTG96QOxw*

While I cannot offer a complete proof at this time, I hope this information provides some insight into the fascinating world of Goldbach's Conjecture and the ongoing efforts to solve it.

EXAMPLE 5

User: Is there life after death, and how does it compare with life on Earth?

Bard: The question of life after death is a profound one that has been pondered by humanity for millennia. There is no scientific consensus on the matter, as it is not something that can be directly observed or measured. However, various religions and philosophical perspectives offer different beliefs and theories about what, if anything, might exist beyond our physical lives.

Here are some of the major perspectives on life after death:

Religious Perspectives:

- **Abrahamic Religions:** Christianity, Islam, and Judaism all believe in some form of afterlife, where individuals are judged based on their actions in this life and rewarded or punished accordingly. The specific details of these afterlife realms vary across these religions.
- **Eastern Religions:** Hinduism, Buddhism, and Jainism believe in reincarnation, where the soul is reborn into another physical body after

death. The karma accumulated in previous lives determines the nature of the next life.

- **Indigenous Religions:** Many indigenous cultures around the world hold diverse beliefs about the afterlife, often involving the continuation of the spirit in a spiritual world or the interconnectedness of the living and the dead.

Philosophical Perspectives:

- **Materialism:** This view holds that consciousness is a product of the brain and ceases to exist after death. Therefore, there is no life after death in the traditional sense.
- **Dualism:** This view suggests that the mind and body are separate entities, with the mind potentially surviving the death of the body. This opens the possibility for some form of afterlife.
- **Near-Death Experiences (NDEs):** Some people who have had NDEs report experiencing a sense of peace, out-of-body experiences, and encounters with deceased loved ones. These experiences are often cited as evidence of an afterlife, but they can also be explained by physiological or psychological factors.

It is important to note that these are just a few of the many perspectives on life after death. Ultimately, the question of what, if anything, lies beyond our physical lives remains a mystery.

Comparing life after death with life on Earth is difficult, as we lack concrete information about what the afterlife might be like. However, based on various beliefs and theories, some potential differences include:

- **Immateriality:** In some afterlife scenarios, individuals may exist as noncorporeal beings, free from the limitations of a physical body.
- **Timelessness:** Time may not exist in the same way as it does on Earth, possibly allowing for experiences outside of our linear perception of time.
- **Knowledge and Understanding:** The afterlife may provide access to greater knowledge and understanding of the universe and ourselves.
- **Connections with Deceased Loved Ones:** Some beliefs suggest the possibility of reuniting with deceased loved ones in the afterlife.

Ultimately, the question of life after death is a personal one. Each individual must decide for themselves what they believe based on their own values, experiences, and understanding of the world.

It is important to respect diverse perspectives on this sensitive topic and avoid making claims of absolute certainty. While we may never have definitive answers about life after death, the continued exploration of this question can provide comfort, hope, and a sense of purpose for many.

Bard may display inaccurate info, including about people, so double-check its responses. Your privacy & Bard.

NOTE *As you can see from the preceding examples, Bard provides impressive and accurate responses to queries in a manner that surpasses many chatbots of recent years. However, it is still possible to confound this Bard (which is true of other chatbots as well).*

ALTERNATIVES TO BARD

There are several alternatives to Bard that offer a similar set of features, some of which are listed below:

- Bing Chat
- ChatGPT/GPT4
- Jasper
- PaLM (Google)
- Pi
- POE (LinkedIn)
- Replika
- WriteSonic
- YouChat

The following subsections discuss some (but not all) of the Bard alternatives in the preceding list.

YouChat

One alternative to Bard is YouChat, which is part of the search engine *you.com*. It is accessible at *https://you.com/*.

Richard Socher, who is well known in the ML community for his many contributions, is the creator of *you.com*. According to Socher, YouChat is a search engine that can provide the usual search-related functionality, as well as the ability to search the Web to obtain more information and provide responses to queries from users.

Another competitor is POE from LinkedIn, and you can create a free account at *https://poe.com/login*.

Pi from Inflection

Pi is a chatbot developed by Inflection, which is a company that was started by Mustafa Suleyman, who is also the founder of DeepMind. Pi is accessible at *https://pi.ai/talk*. More information about Pi can be found online:

https://medium.com/@ignacio.de.gregorio.noblejas/meet-pi-Bards-newest-rival-and-the-most-human-ai-in-the-world-367b461c0af1

The development team used Reinforcement Learning from Human Feedback (RLHF) in order to train this chatbot:

https://medium.com/@ignacio.de.gregorio.noblejas/meet-pi-chatgpts-newest-rival-and-the-most-human-ai-in-the-world-367b461c0af1

Shortly after the release of ChatGPT on November 30, 2022, there was a flurry of activity among various companies to release a competitor to ChatGPT, which arguably are also competitors to Bard, some of which are listed below:

- CoPilot (Microsoft)
- Codex (OpenAI)
- Apple GPT (Apple)
- Claude 2 (Anthropic)
- Llama-2 (Meta)

The following subsections contain additional details regarding the LLMs in the preceding list.

CoPilot (OpenAI/Microsoft)

Microsoft CoPilot is a Visual Studio Code extension that is also powered by GPT-4. GitHub CoPilot is already known for its ability to generate blocks of code within the context of a program. In addition, Microsoft is also developing Microsoft 365 CoPilot, whose availability date has not been announced as of mid-2023.

However, Microsoft has provided early demos that show some of the capabilities of Microsoft 365 CoPilot, which includes automating tasks such as

- writing emails
- summarizing meetings
- making PowerPoint presentations

Microsoft 365 CoPilot can analyze data in Excel spreadsheets, insert AI-generated images in PowerPoint, and generate drafts of cover letters. Microsoft has also integrated Microsoft 365 CoPilot into some of its existing products, such as Loop and OneNote.

According to the following article, Microsoft intends to charge $30 per month for Office 365 Copilot:

https://www.extremetech.com/extreme/microsoft-to-charge-30-per-month-for-ai-powered-office-apps

Copilot was reverse engineered in late 2022, which is described online:

https://thakkarparth007.github.io/copilot-explorer/posts/copilot-internals

The following article shows you how to create a GPT-3 application that uses NextJS, React, and CoPilot:

https://github.blog/2023-07-25-how-to-build-a-gpt-3-app-with-nextjs-react-and-github-copilot/

Codex (OpenAI)

OpenAI Codex is a fine-tuned GPT3-based LLM that generates code from text. Codex powers GitHub Copilot (discussed in the preceding section). Codex was trained on more than 150 GB of Python code that was obtained from more than 50 million GitHub repositories.

According to OpenAI, the primary purpose of Codex is to accelerate human programming, and it can complete almost 40% of requests. Codex tends to work quite well for generating code for solving simple tasks. Navigate to the Codex home page to obtain more information: *https://openai.com/blog/openai-codex*.

Apple GPT

In mid-2023, Apple announced Apple GPT, which is a competitor to Bard from OpenAI. The actual release date was projected to be 2024. "Apple GPT" is the current name for a product that is intended to compete with Google Bard, OpenAI Bard, and Microsoft Bing AI.

In brief, the LLM PaLM 2 powers Google Bard, and GPT-4 powers Bard as well as Bing Chat, whereas Ajax is what powers Apple GPT. Ajax is based on Jax from Google, and the name Ajax is a clever concatenation ("Apple Jax," perhaps?).

Claude 2

Anthropic created the LLM Claude 2. Claude 2 can not only answer queries about specific topics, but can also perform searches that involve multiple documents, summarize documents, create documents, and generate code.

Claude 2 is an improvement on Anthropic's predecessor Claude 1.3, and it can ingest entire books as well as generate code based on prompts from users. Claude 2 appears to be comparable with its rivals Bard and GPT-4 in terms of competing functionality.

Claude 2 supports a context window of 100,000 tokens. Moreover, Claude 2 was trained on data as recent as early 2023, whereas Bard was trained on data up until 2021. However, Claude 2 cannot search the Web (unlike its competitor GPT-4). Stay tuned to Anthropic, where you will probably see more good things in the LLM space.

SUMMARY

This chapter started with a discussion of generative AI, along with some of the major companies in this arena, such as Google, OpenAI, Cohere, and Hugging Face.

In addition, you learned about prompt engineering, which addresses the various ways that you can design the content of the prompts that you provide to an LLM.

Next, you learned about Google Gemini and some of its features, and read a brief comparison of Gemini Ultra with GPT-4 from OpenAI.

CHAPTER 6

BARD AND DATA VISUALIZATION

This chapter contains examples of using Bard in order to perform data visualization, such as charts and graphs that are based on datasets (e.g., the Titanic dataset). Note that Bard generated all the code samples as well as the explanation of the code samples.

The first part of this chapter contains an extensive section regarding various types of charts and graphs (such as bar charts, line graphs, histograms, and so forth), along with their advantages and disadvantages. This section also contains Bard-generated Python code for rendering charts and graphs.

The second part of this chapter contains examples of data visualization with `Matplotlib`, where the code samples were generated with Bard. The third part of this chapter contains examples of data visualization with Seaborn, where the code samples were generated with Bard.

A suggestion: after you have read the material in this chapter, it would be interesting to compare the code samples in this chapter with the code samples in Chapter 3 as well as Chapter 4.

WORKING WITH CHARTS AND GRAPHS

Each chart type has its unique strengths and is best suited for specific kinds of data and analysis. The choice of chart often depends on the nature of the data and the specific insights one wants to derive. This section contains multiple subsections that provide information about an assortment of charts and graphs, as shown here:

```
Bar Charts
Pie Charts
Line Graphs
Heatmap
Histogram
Box Plot
Pareto Chart
```

```
Radar Chart
Treemap
Waterfall Chart
Scatter Plots
```

Each of the charts and graphs in the preceding bullet list are discussed in the following subsections.

Bar Charts

Bar charts represent data with rectangular bars. The lengths of the bars are proportional to the values they represent. They can be vertical (column charts) or horizontal. An example of Usage involves Comparing the sales of different products in a store.

Some advantages of bar charts are listed here:

- They are easily interpretable and widely recognized.
- They allow for comparison of individual or multiple data series.
- They are effective for displaying data that spans several categories.

Some disadvantages of bar charts are listed here:

- They are not ideal for showing patterns or trends over time.
- They can become cluttered when comparing too many categories.

Pie Charts

Pie charts represent data in a circular format, with individual sections (slices) showing categories' proportion to the whole. An example of Usage involves Representing market share of different companies in an industry.

Some advantages of pie charts are listed here:

- They include simple visualization that shows part-to-whole relationships.
- They clearly indicate proportions.
- They are effective when there are a limited number of categories.

Some disadvantages of pie charts are listed here:

- They are not efficient for comparing individual categories.
- They can become ineffective and hard to interpret with too many slices.
- They only show proportions and not absolute values.

Line Graphs

Line graphs display data points connected by straight lines. They are used primarily to visualize values over a continuous interval or time period. An example of Usage involves Tracking a company's revenue growth over several years.

Some advantages of line graphs are listed as follows:

- They are effective for displaying trends over time.
- They allow for comparison of multiple data series on one graph.
- They display clear visualization of data points and intervals.

Some disadvantages of line graphs are listed as follows:

- They are not suitable for showing part-to-whole relationships.
- They can become cluttered when displaying too many data series.
- They require a meaningful order of data points.

Heatmap

A heatmap represents data in a matrix format, where individual values are depicted as colors. The color intensity usually represents the magnitude of the value. An example of Usage involves Visualizing Web site visitor activity on different parts of a Web page.

Some advantages of heatmaps are listed here:

- They quickly identify patterns, correlations, and areas of concentration.
- They use color effectively to convey information about magnitudes.

Some disadvantages of heatmaps are listed as follows:

- They are not suitable for detailed numerical analysis.
- Color choices are crucial (poor choices can mislead interpretation).

Histogram

A histogram is a graphical representation of the distribution of a dataset. It's an estimate of the probability distribution of a continuous variable. An example of Usage involves Showing the distribution of ages in a population.

Some advantages of histograms are listed here:

- They provide a visual interpretation of numerical data by indicating the number of data points that lie within a range of values.
- They can help identify data distribution patterns.

Some disadvantages of histograms are listed as follows:

- They do not show exact values.
- The amount of and width of bins can influence perception.

Box Plot

Represents a summary of a dataset using quartiles. The "box" shows the interquartile range, while the "whiskers" indicates variability outside the upper and lower quartiles. An example of Usage involves Comparing sales performances across different teams.

Some advantages of box plots are listed here:

- Allows for quick visualization of data spread and skewness.
- They identify outliers.

Some disadvantages of box plots are listed as follows:

- They are not suitable for detailed distribution analysis.
- They do not show the frequency distribution of data.

Pareto Chart

A Pareto chart combines a bar chart and a line graph to represent the cumulative frequency of occurrences. It identifies the most significant factors in a dataset. An example of Usage involves Identifying which product defects occur most frequently.

Some advantages of Pareto charts are listed here:

- They efficiently highlight the most important factors in large datasets.
- They aid in prioritizing efforts.

Some disadvantages of Pareto charts are listed here:

- They are limited to datasets where ranking and prioritization are relevant.
- They are not suitable for showing relationships between data points.

Radar Chart

A graphical method of displaying data in a 2D chart of three or more quantitative variables. The data points are plotted on axes that start from the center. An example of Usage involves Comparing the performance metrics of products.

Some advantages of radar charts are listed as follows:

- It's possible to compare multiple quantitative variables.
- They provides a visual overview of the data.

Some disadvantages of radar charts are listed here:

- They can become cluttered when comparing too many datasets.
- They are difficult to interpret with information representing similar values.

Treemap

A treemap displays hierarchical data as nested rectangles. Each branch of the hierarchy is represented by colored rectangles. An example of Usage involves Visualizing storage usage on a computer.

Some advantages of tree maps are listed here:

- They show an efficient use of space.
- They can represent multiple dimensions using size and color.

Some disadvantages of tree maps are listed as follows:

- They are most suitable for datasets with large hierarchies.
- They are sometimes difficult to interpret.

Waterfall Chart

A waterfall chart represents the cumulative effect of sequentially occurring positive or negative values. An example of Usage involves Visualizing how profit or revenue is affected by various factors.

Some advantages of waterfall charts are listed here:

- They clearly visualize positive and negative sequential changes.
- They help in understanding the gradual transition from one data point to another.

Some disadvantages of waterfall charts are listed as follows:

- They are limited to situations where understanding sequential changes is necessary.
- They sometimes include too many data points and can become confusing.

LINE PLOTS WITH MATPLOTLIB

The following prompt was submitted to Bard in order to generate `Python` code for this section:

```
Please generate Python code for a simple line graph along
with an explanation of the code.
```

Listing 6.1 displays the contents of `line_plot.py` that Bard generated in order to render a line using `Matplotlib`.

LISTING 6.1: line_plot.py

```
import matplotlib.pyplot as plt
```

```
# Data for the line (replace with your own data)
x = [1, 2, 3, 4, 5]
y = [3, 5, 7, 2, 1]

# Create the line plot
plt.plot(x, y)

# Add labels and title
plt.xlabel("X-axis")
plt.ylabel("Y-axis")
plt.title("Simple Line Graph")

# Show the plot
plt.show()
```

Bard also generated the following explanation for the code in Listing 6.1.

Explanation:

1. *Import libraries*: We import `matplotlib.pyplot` as `plt` for plotting functionalities.
2. *Data definition*: Define two lists, `x` and `y`, containing the data points for the X and Y axes. Replace these with your own data.
3. *Line plot creation*: Use `plt.plot(x, y)` to create a line plot with the data points from `x` and `y`.
4. *Labels and title*: Set labels for the X and Y axes using `plt.xlabel` and `plt.ylabel` with appropriate text. Set a title using `plt.title` with your desired title.
5. *Show the plot*: Use `plt.show()` to display the created line graph on your screen.

This is a basic example of a line graph in `Python`. You can customize it further by:

- *Changing plot style*: Use different line styles or markers with `line style` and `marker` arguments in `plt.plot`.
- *Adding grid lines*: Use `plt.grid(True)` to enable grid lines for reference.
- *Customizing axes*: Set specific ranges for the axes using `plt.xlim` and `plt.ylim`.
- *Adding legends*: Use `plt.legend` to differentiate multiple lines on the same plot.

Remember to adjust the data and styling options based on your specific needs and the characteristics of your data. I hope this helps! Let me know if you have any other questions.

Figure 6.1 displays the graph that is generated by launching the code in Listing 6.1.

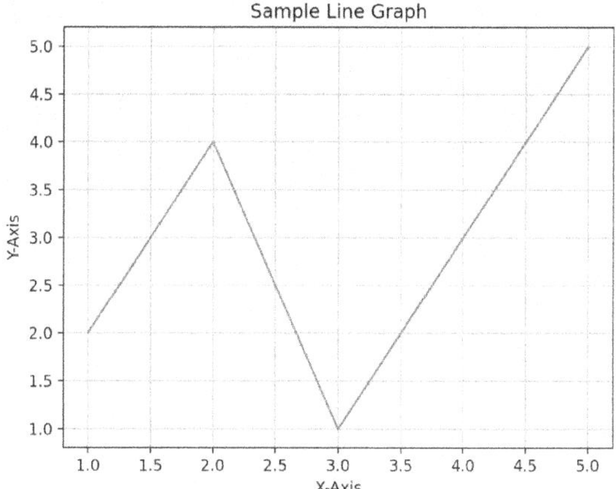

FIGURE 6.1. A line plot with Matplotlib.

A PIE CHART USING MATPLOTLIB

Pie charts are ideal for displaying proportional data among categories. The pie function from Matplotlib provides an easy way to achieve this. The following prompt was submitted to Bard in order to generate `Python` code for this section:

```
Please generate Python code for a pie chart along with an
explanation of the code.
```

Listing 6.2 displays the contents of `pie_chart1.py` that Bard generated in order to render a line using `Matplotlib`.

LISTING 6.2: pie_chart1.py

```
import matplotlib.pyplot as plt

# Pie chart data (replace with your own)
data = [30, 40, 20, 10]
labels = ["Category 1", "Category 2", "Category 3", "Category 4"]

# Create the pie chart
plt.pie(data, labels=labels, autopct="%1.1f%%")

# Customize the pie chart (optional)
plt.title("Pie Chart Example")
plt.legend(loc="best")

# Show the plot
plt.show()
```

Explanation:

1. *Import libraries*: We import `matplotlib.pyplot` as `plt` for plotting functionalities.
2. *Data definition*: Define two lists, `data` and `labels`. `data` contains the values for each slice of the pie chart, and `labels` contains the corresponding labels for each slice. Replace these with your own data and labels.
3. *Pie chart creation*: Use `plt.pie(data, labels=labels)` to create a pie chart with the data and labels provided.
4. *Autopct (optional)*: Add `autopct="%1.1f%%"` to display the percentage value of each slice next to it with one decimal point precision.
5. *Customize chart (optional)*: Add a title using `plt.title` and configure the legend placement using `plt.legend(loc="best")`.
6. *Show the plot*: Use `plt.show()` to display the created pie chart on your screen.

Customization options:

- Change the slice colors with `plt.pie(data, labels=labels, colors=["red", "green", "blue", "yellow"])`.
- Explode specific slices for emphasis using `plt.pie(data, labels=labels, explode=[0.1, 0, 0, 0])`.
- Adjust the pie chart radius with `plt.pie(data, labels=labels, radius=0.5)`.
- Modify the appearance of the legend with various `plt.legend` arguments.

Remember to adapt the data, labels, and customization options to match your specific data and desired aesthetics.

Figure 6.2 displays the pie chart that is rendered by launching the code in Listing 6.2.

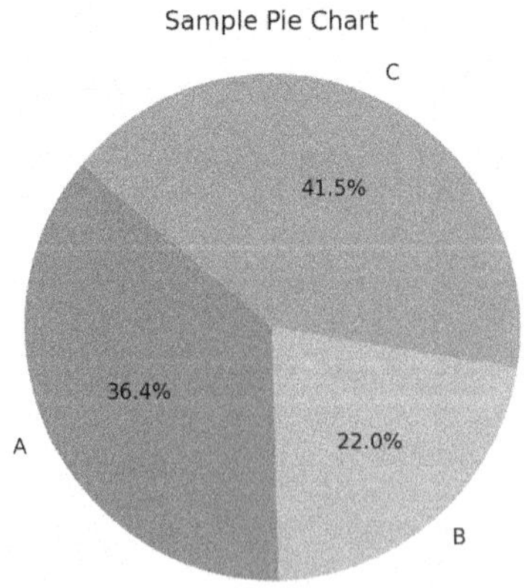

FIGURE 6.2. A pie chart with Matplotlib.

BOX AND WHISKER PLOTS USING MATPLOTLIB

Box plots, or box-and-whisker plots, provide a summary of the distribution of data, highlighting the central tendency, variability, and presence of outliers. They can be particularly useful for comparing distributions across different groups. Display the distribution of data based on the minimum, first quartile, median, third quartile, and maximum.

The following prompt was submitted to Bard in order to generate `Python` code for this section:

```
Please generate Python code for a box plot chart along with
an explanation of the code.
```

Listing 6.3 displays the contents of `boxplot1.py` that Bard generated in order to render a box plot.

LISTING 6.3: boxplot1.py

```
import matplotlib.pyplot as plt

# Data for each group (replace with your own)
data1 = [5, 7, 3, 8, 2, 1, 4, 9]
data2 = [6, 4, 10, 5, 2, 8, 3, 7]

# Create the box plot
plt.boxplot([data1, data2], labels=["Group 1", "Group 2"])

# Customize the plot (optional)
plt.xlabel("Groups")
plt.ylabel("Values")
plt.title("Box Plot Comparison")
plt.grid(True)

# Show the plot
plt.show()
```

Explanation:

1. *Import libraries*: We import `matplotlib.pyplot` as `plt` for plotting functionalities.
2. *Data definition*: Define two lists, `data1` and `data2`, containing the data points for each group you want to compare. Replace them with your own data.
3. *Box plot creation*: Use `plt.boxplot([data1, data2], labels=["Group 1", "Group 2"])` to create a box plot with the data and labels provided.
4. *Customize the plot (optional)*: Set labels for the X and Y axes using `plt.xlabel` and `plt.ylabel`. Set a title using `plt.title`. Enable grid lines for reference using `plt.grid(True)`.
5. *Show the plot*: Use `plt.show()` to display the box plot created on your screen.

Customization options:

- Change box colors and styles using `boxprops` dictionary arguments within `plt.boxplot`.
- Adjust whisker lengths and notch settings for the box.
- Add additional data groups and customize their labels.
- Modify the plot layout and legend appearance.

Remember to adapt the data, labels, and customization options to fit your specific data and desired representation.

Figure 6.3 displays the box plot that is rendered by launching the code in Listing 6.3.

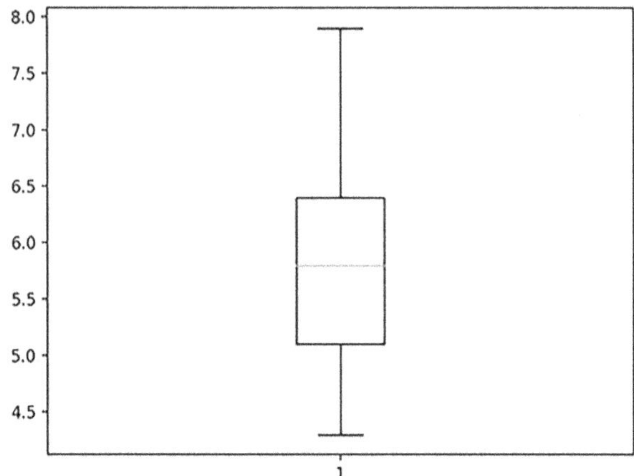

FIGURE 6.3. A box plot with Matplotlib.

STACKED BAR CHARTS WITH MATPLOTLIB

Stacked bar charts allow for the representation of subgroups in each category, giving a sense of the total size across categories and the sub-group distributions within them. The following prompt was submitted to Bard in order to generate `Python` code for this section:

```
Please generate Python code for a stacked bar chart along
with an explanation of the code.
```

Listing 6.4 displays the contents of `stacked_bar_charts.py` that Bard generated in order to render stacked bar charts using `Matplotlib`.

LISTING 6.4: stacked_bar_charts.py

```
import matplotlib.pyplot as plt

# Define data for each category and group (replace with your
own)
```

```
categories = ["Category 1", "Category 2", "Category 3"]
data1 = [3, 5, 7]  # Group 1 values for each category
data2 = [2, 1, 4]  # Group 2 values for each category

# Create the stacked bar chart
plt.figure(figsize=(8, 6))  # Adjust figure size if needed
bar_width = 0.35
index = range(len(categories))  # Positions for category bars

p1 = plt.bar(index, data1, bar_width, label="Group 1")
p2 = plt.bar([i + bar_width for i in index], data2, bar_
width, label="Group 2", bottom=data1)

# Customize the plot
plt.xlabel("Categories")
plt.ylabel("Value")
plt.title("Stacked Bar Chart")
plt.xticks([i + bar_width / 2 for i in index], categories)
# Set category labels
plt.legend()
plt.grid(axis="y")

# Show the plot
plt.tight_layout()
plt.show()
```

Explanation:

1. *Import libraries*: We import `matplotlib.pyplot` as `plt` for plotting functionalities.
2. *Data definition*: Define two lists, `categories` for the X-axis labels and `data1`, `data2` for the data points of each group within each category. Replace these with your own data.
3. *Bar creation*:
   - Define the bar width and positions on the X-axis for each category.
   - Use `plt.bar` twice to create separate bars for each group on top of each other, specifying their data, width, position, and bottom base for the stacked layout.
4. *Customization*:
   - Add labels and title for the plot.
   - Set category labels on the X-axis using their positions and the defined categories list.
   - Display a legend for each group.
   - Enable grid lines on the Y-axis for reference.
5. *Show the plot*: Use `plt.tight_layout` to adjust spacing and `plt.show()` to display the stacked bar chart.

Customization options:

- Change bar colors and styles for each group.
- Add error bars to represent data variability.
- Adjust bar width and spacing between categories.
- Annotate specific bars with values or text labels.
- Stack more groups or categories based on your data structure.

Remember to adapt the data, styling, and customizations based on your specific data and the desired representation of your stacked bar chart.

Figure 6.4 displays the stacked bar charts that are rendered by launching the code in Listing 6.4.

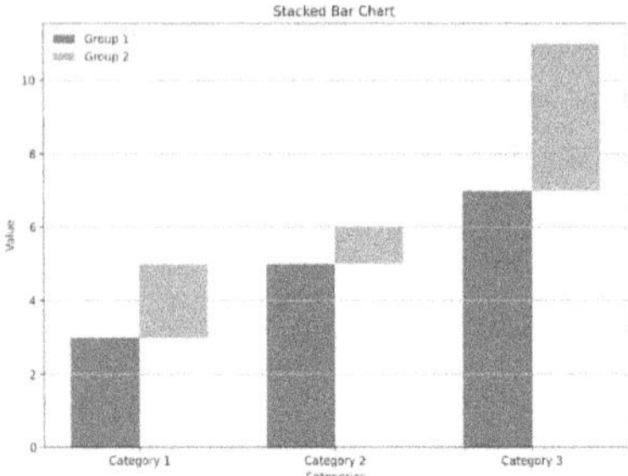

FIGURE 6.4. Stacked bar chart.

DONUT CHART USING MATPLOTLIB

Donut charts are a variation of pie charts. The hollow center can be used for additional annotations or just to provide a different aesthetic. Represent data proportionally among categories, similar to a pie chart but with a hollow center. The following prompt was submitted to Bard in order to generate `Python` code for this section:

```
Please generate Python code for a doughnut chart along with
an explanation of the code.
```

Listing 6.5 displays the contents of `donut_charts.py` that Bard generated in order to render a donut chart using `Matplotlib`.

LISTING 6.5: donut_charts.py

```
import matplotlib.pyplot as plt

# Data for each slice (replace with your own)
data = [30, 50, 15, 5]
labels = ["Category 1", "Category 2", "Category 3", "Category 4"]
```

```
# Create the doughnut chart
plt.figure(figsize=(8, 8))  # Adjust size if needed
plt.pie(data, labels=labels, autopct="%1.1f%%",
startangle=140)  # Use startangle for "donut hole"

# Customize the plot (optional)
plt.axis("equal")  # Equal aspect ratio for circular chart
plt.title("Doughnut Chart Example")
plt.legend(loc="best")

# Show the plot
plt.show()
```

Explanation:

1. *Import libraries*: We import `matplotlib.pyplot` as `plt` for plotting functionalities.
2. *Data definition*: Define two lists, `data` containing values for each slice of the doughnut and `labels` for the corresponding slice labels. Replace them with your own data and labels.
3. *Doughnut chart creation*:
   - Use `plt.figure` to set the figure size (square for doughnuts).
   - Use `plt.pie` with the provided data, labels, and additional arguments:
   - `autopct="%1.1f%%"`: Displays percentage values on each slice with one decimal point precision.
   - `startangle=140`: Rotates the starting angle of the first slice to create a "donut hole" effect.
4. *Customization (optional)*:
   - Set `plt.axis("equal")` to ensure a circular shape for the doughnut.
   - Add a title using `plt.title`.
   - Configure the legend placement with `plt.legend(loc="best")`.
5. *Show the plot*: Use `plt.show()` to display the created doughnut chart.

Further customization options:

- Change slice colors and styles using `plt.pie(data, labels=labels, colors=["red", "green", "blue", "yellow"])`.
- Vary slice thicknesses with `plt.pie(data, labels=labels, autopct="%1.1f%%", radius=1, wedgeprops=dict(width=0.6))`.
- Add a hole in the center without rotation using `plt.pie(data, labels=labels, autopct="%1.1f%%", radius=1, hole=True)`.
- Explore different legend styles and annotations for detailed representation.

Remember to adapt the data, formatting, and customizations based on your specific data and desired visual appearance of your doughnut chart.

Figure 6.5 displays the donut chart that is rendered by launching the code in Listing 6.5.

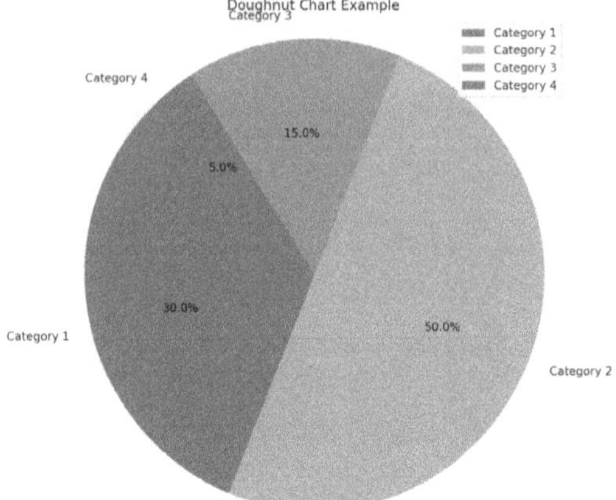

FIGURE 6.5. Doughnut chart.

3D SURFACE PLOTS WITH MATPLOTLIB

3D surface plots are used for visualizing functions with two variables. They can reveal intricate patterns and relationships in the data. The following prompt was submitted to Bard in order to generate `Python` code for this section:

```
Please generate Python code for a 3D surface chart along
with an explanation of the code.
```

Listing 6.6 displays the contents of `3d_surface.py` that Bard generated in order to render a 3D surface using `mpl_toolkits`. Incidentally, if you encounter issues with `mpl_toolkits`, please read the following post that contains useful information:

https://stackoverflow.com/questions/37661119/python-mpl-toolkits-installation-issue

LISTING 6.6: 3d_surface.py

```
import matplotlib.pyplot as plt
from mpl_toolkits.mplot3d import Axes3D

# Define your function (replace with your own)
def my_function(x, y):
    # Example mathematical function
    return np.sin(x) * np.cos(y)

# Generate data points
x = np.linspace(-2, 2, 100)
y = np.linspace(-2, 2, 100)
```

```
# Create a mesh grid from the data points
X, Y = np.meshgrid(x, y)

# Calculate Z values based on your function
Z = my_function(X, Y)

# Create the 3D surface plot
fig = plt.figure(figsize=(8, 6))
ax = fig.add_subplot(111, projection="3d")
surf = ax.plot_surface(X, Y, Z, cmap="coolwarm")  # Change
cmap for different color gradients

# Customize the plot (optional)
ax.set_xlabel("X-axis")
ax.set_ylabel("Y-axis")
ax.set_zlabel("Z-axis")
ax.set_title("3D Surface Plot")
ax.set_xticks([-2, 0, 2])  # Set specific tick marks if needed
ax.set_yticks([-2, 0, 2])
ax.set_zlim(-1, 1)  # Adjust Z-axis limits

# Add a colorbar (optional)
fig.colorbar(surf, label="Z-value")

# Show the plot
plt.show()
```

Explanation:

1. *Import libraries*: We import `matplotlib.pyplot` as `plt` for plotting and `Axes3D` from `mpl_toolkits` for 3D functionalities.
2. *Define function*: Replace `my_function(x, y)` with your desired mathematical function or data source that maps X and Y values to Z values for the surface.
3. *Generate data points*: Define grids of X and Y values using `np.linspace` to cover the desired range of the surface.
4. *Create mesh grid*: Use `np.meshgrid` to combine the X and Y grids into a mesh used for plotting the surface.
5. *Calculate Z values*: Apply your function to the X and Y mesh grid to generate the corresponding Z values for each point on the surface.
6. *3D surface plot*:
   - Create a figure and a 3D subplot using `plt.figure` and `fig.add_subplot`.
   - Use `ax.plot_surface(X, Y, Z, cmap="coolwarm")` to plot the surface from the X, Y, and Z data, specifying a colormap for visualization.
7. Customization (optional):

- Add labels for each axis and title for the plot using `ax.set_*`.
- Adjust tick marks and Z-axis limits for clarity.
- Add a colorbar for the Z values using `fig.colorbar`.

8. Show the plot: Use `plt.show()` to display the created 3D surface chart.

Further customization options:

- Change the surface shading and wireframe visibility using additional arguments in `ax.plot_surface`.
- Set the viewing angle with `ax.view_init(elev=15, azim=-60)`.
- Modify the colormap scheme.
- Add legends or annotations for specific features on the surface.
- Explore different lighting effects for enhanced realism.

Remember to adapt the function, data generation, and customization options to match your specific data and desired appearance of the 3D surface chart.

Launch the code in Listing 6.6 and you will see the 3D surface that is displayed in Figure 6.6.

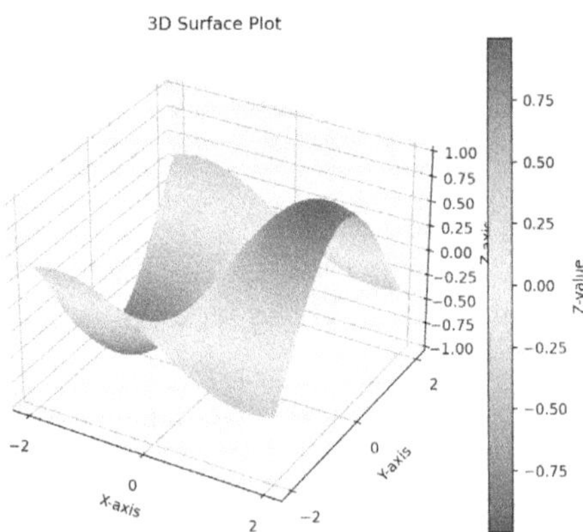

FIGURE 6.6. A 3D surface with Matplotlib.

MATPLOTLIB'S CONTOUR PLOTS

Contour plots help visualize three-dimensional data in two dimensions using contour lines. Each contour line represents points of equal value. Visualize contour lines for three-dimensional data. The following prompt was submitted to Bard in order to generate `Python` code for this section:

```
Please generate Python code for a contour plot along with
an explanation of the code.
```

Listing 6.7 displays the contents of `contour_lines.py` that Bard generated in order to render contour lines using Matplotlib.

LISTING 6.7: contour_lines.py

```
import matplotlib.pyplot as plt
import numpy as np

# Define your function (replace with your own)
def my_function(x, y):
    # Example mathematical function
    return np.sin(x) * np.cos(y)

# Generate data points
x = np.linspace(-2, 2, 100)
y = np.linspace(-2, 2, 100)

# Create a mesh grid from the data points
X, Y = np.meshgrid(x, y)

# Calculate Z values based on your function
Z = my_function(X, Y)

# Create the contour plot
fig, ax = plt.subplots()
levels = np.linspace(-1, 1, 15)  # Adjust number of levels for
detail
contour = ax.contour(X, Y, Z, levels=levels,
cmap="coolwarm")  # Change cmap for different color
gradients

# Customize the plot (optional)
ax.set_xlabel("X-axis")
ax.set_ylabel("Y-axis")
ax.set_title("Contour Plot")
ax.clabel(contour, levels=levels, inline=True, fmt="%1.1f")
# Show values on contour lines

# Add a colorbar (optional)
fig.colorbar(contour, label="Z-value")

# Show the plot
plt.show()
```

Explanation:

1. *Import libraries*: We import `matplotlib.pyplot` as `plt` for plotting and `numpy` for math operations.
2. *Define function*: Replace `my_function(x, y)` with your desired mathematical function or data source that maps X and Y values to Z values for the contour plot.
3. *Generate data points*: Define grids of X and Y values using `np.linspace` to cover the desired range of the plot.
4. *Create mesh grid*: Use `np.meshgrid` to combine the X and Y grids into a mesh used for calculations and plotting.

5. *Calculate Z values*: Apply your function to the X and Y mesh grid to generate the corresponding Z values for each point on the grid.
6. *Contour plot creation*:
   - Create a figure and an axes object using `plt.subplots()`.
   - Use `ax.contour(X, Y, Z, levels=levels, cmap="coolwarm")` to draw contour lines based on the Z values at different levels, specify the number of levels for detail, and choose a colormap for visualization.
7. *Customization (optional)*:
   - Add labels for each axis and title for the plot using `ax.set_*`.
   - Show values on contour lines with `ax.clabel(contour, levels=levels, inline=True, fmt="%1.1f")`, specifying levels and formatting.
   - Add a colorbar for the Z values using `fig.colorbar`.
8. *Show the plot*: Use `plt.show()` to display the created contour plot.

Further customization options:

- Change the line styles and thicknesses of contour lines using `contour.set_linewidths` and `contour.set_line styles`.
- Fill areas between contour lines with `ax.contourf(X, Y, Z, levels=levels, cmap="coolwarm")`.
- Add hatching or stippling to filled areas.
- Modify the z-order and transparency of different plot elements.
- Explore different interpolation methods for smoother contours.

Remember to adapt the function, data generation, and customization options to match your specific data and desired appearance of the contour plot.

Figure 6.7 displays the contour plot that is rendered by launching the code in Listing 6.7.

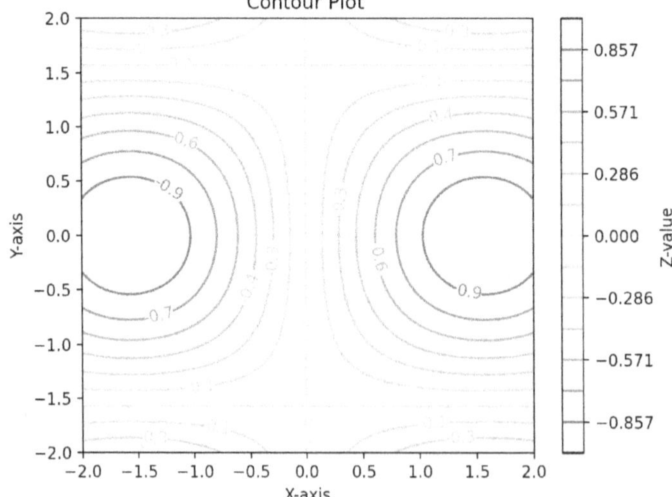

FIGURE 6.7. Contour plot.

STREAMPLOT FOR VECTOR FIELDS

Streamplots are used for displaying vector fields, like wind patterns. They provide a snapshot of the flow trajectories and can be color-coded for scalar data. Visualize a vector field as streamlines. The following prompt was submitted to Bard in order to generate `Python` code for this section:

```
Please generate Python code for a stream plot along with an
explanation of the code.
```

Listing 6.8 displays the contents of `stream_plot.py` that Bard generated in order to render a stream plot using `Seaborn`.

LISTING 6.8: stream_plot.py

```
import matplotlib.pyplot as plt
import numpy as np

# Define vector field function
def u(x, y):
  return np.pi * np.cos(np.pi * x) * np.sin(np.pi * y)

def v(x, y):
  return -np.pi * np.sin(np.pi * x) * np.cos(np.pi * y)

# Generate data points
x = np.linspace(-2, 2, 100)
y = np.linspace(-2, 2, 100)

# Calculate u and v values at each point
u_vals = u(np.outer(x, np.ones_like(y)), np.outer(np.ones_
like(x), y))
v_vals = v(np.outer(x, np.ones_like(y)), np.outer(np.ones_
like(x), y))

# Create the stream plot
fig, ax = plt.subplots()
stream = ax.streamplot(x, y, u_vals, v_vals, linewidth=2,
arrowsize=10, density=2)

# Customize the plot (optional)
ax.set_xlabel("X-axis")
ax.set_ylabel("Y-axis")
ax.set_title("Stream Plot")
ax.set_xlim(-2, 2)
ax.set_ylim(-2, 2)

# Show the plot
plt.show()
```

Explanation:

1. *Import libraries*: We import `matplotlib.pyplot` as `plt` for plotting and `numpy` for mathematical operations.
2. *Define vector field function*: Replace `u(x, y)` and `v(x, y)` with your desired vector field functions that define the direction and magnitude of the flow at each point in the plane. In this example, we use a simple function that creates swirling streamlines.
3. *Generate data points*: Define grids of X and Y values using `np.linspace` to cover the desired area of the plot.
4. *Calculate u and v values*: Apply the vector field functions to the X and Y grids to calculate the corresponding u and v values for each point.
5. *Stream plot creation*:
   - Create a figure and an axes object using `plt.subplots()`.
   - Use `ax.streamplot(x, y, u_vals, v_vals, linewidth=2, arrowsize=10, density=2)` to draw streamlines based on the u and v values at each point, specifying line width, arrow size, and density for visual clarity.
6. *Customization (optional)*:
   - Add labels for each axis and title for the plot using `ax.set_*`.
   - Adjust plot limits and other visual properties.
7. *Show the plot*: Use `plt.show()` to display the created stream plot.

This code will generate a visual representation of the flow defined by your vector field.

Customization options:

- Change the line style and color of the streamlines.
- Vary the arrow size and density along the streamlines.
- Overlay the streamlines on another plot, such as a contour plot or heatmap.
- Add annotations or text labels to highlight specific features of the flow.

Remember to adapt the vector field functions, data generation, and customization options to match your specific data and desired appearance of the stream plot.

Figure 6.8 displays the stream plot that is rendered by launching the code in Listing 6.8.

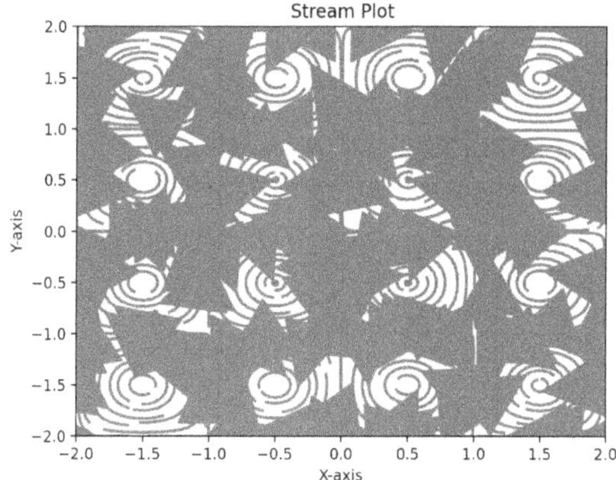

FIGURE 6.8. Stream plot.

POLAR PLOTS

Polar plots or radial plots are suitable for displaying multivariate data in a two-dimensional chart where the variables are represented on axes starting from the same point. They're great for viewing patterns based on angles and magnitudes. Display data in terms of values and angles. The following prompt was submitted to Bard in order to generate `Python` code for this section:

```
Please generate Python code for a polar plot along with an
explanation of the code.
```

Listing 6.9 displays the contents of `polar_plots.py` that Bard generated in order to render stacked bar charts using Seaborn.

LISTING 6.9: polar_plots.py

```
import matplotlib.pyplot as plt
Import numpy as np # Bard forgot this code snippet

# Define data for each theta value (replace with your own)
theta = np.linspace(0, 2*np.pi, 100)  # Angles from 0 to 2π
radius = np.sin(2 * theta) + 2        # Example data based
                                        on theta

# Create the polar plot
fig, ax = plt.subplots(subplot_kw=dict(projection="polar"))
ax.plot(theta, radius, marker="o", line style="-",
label="Data")  # Customize style and label

# Customize the plot (optional)
ax.set_title("Polar Plot")
```

```
ax.set_xlabel("Theta")
ax.set_ylabel("Radius")
ax.set_xticks(np.linspace(0, 2*np.pi, 5, endpoint=False))
# Set specific tick marks for theta
ax.set_yticks([1, 2, 3])  # Set specific tick marks for
radius

# Show the plot
plt.legend()
plt.show()
```

Explanation:

1. *Import libraries*: We import `matplotlib.pyplot` as `plt` for plotting functionalities.
2. *Define data*:
   - Define `theta` using `np.linspace` to create an array of angles covering the desired range (usually 0 to 2π for a full circle).
   - Replace `radius` with your actual data points corresponding to each theta value. This could be values from a mathematical function, measurements, or any data associated with angles.
3. *Polar plot creation*:
   - Create a figure and an axes object with the `projection="polar"` keyword argument to specify a polar coordinate system.
   - Use `ax.plot(theta, radius)` to plot the data points as lines or markers connected by lines, specify styling options like marker and line style, and add a label if needed.
4. Customization (optional):
   - Add a title, labels for axes, and adjust tick marks using `ax.set_*` methods.
   - Modify styling elements like colors, marker sizes, and line thicknesses.
   - Add additional data series or annotations for informative representation.
5. Show the plot: Use `plt.legend()` to display the legend if labels are set and `plt.show()` to display the created polar plot.

Further customization options:

- Change the plot area extent with `ax.set_theta_zero_location` and `ax.set_theta_direction`.
- Add grid lines with `ax.set_xticks` and `ax.set_yticks`.
- Fill areas between lines or create sector plots with `ax.fill_between`.
- Explore different polar grid styles and background themes.

Remember to adapt the data definition, plot creation, and customizations based on your specific data and desired appearance of your polar plot.

Figure 6.9 displays the point plot that is rendered by launching the code in Listing 6.9.

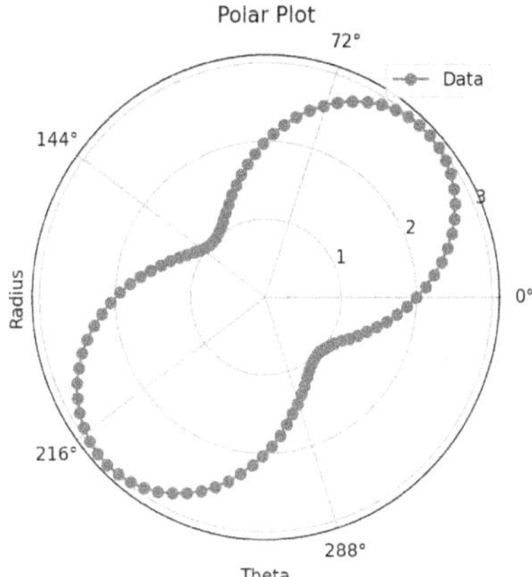

FIGURE 6.9. Polar plots with Matplotlib.

BAR CHARTS

`Seaborn` provides a higher-level interface for `Matplotlib`, making the creation of stylish plots more accessible. This bar plot helps visualize data across different categories. The following prompt was submitted to Bard in order to generate `Python` code for this section:

```
Please generate Python code for a bar plot along with an
explanation of the code.
```

Listing 6.10 displays the contents of `bar_chart1.py` that Bard generated in order to a bar chart using `Seaborn`.

LISTING 6.10: bar_chart1.py

```
import matplotlib.pyplot as plt

# Define data (replace with your own)
categories = ["Category 1", "Category 2", "Category 3"]
data = [5, 7, 3]

# Create the bar plot
plt.figure(figsize=(8, 6))  # adjust figure size if needed
bars = plt.bar(categories, data, color="skyblue")  #
customize bar color

# Add labels and title
plt.xlabel("Categories")
plt.ylabel("Value")
plt.title("Simple Bar Plot")

# Show the plot
plt.show()
```

Explanation:

1. *Import libraries*: We import `matplotlib.pyplot` as `plt` for plotting functionalities.
2. *Define data*:
   - Define a list `categories` with the labels for each bar.
   - Define a list `data` with the corresponding values for each category.
3. *Bar plot creation*:
   - Use `plt.figure` to adjust the figure size if needed.
   - Use `plt.bar(categories, data)` to create the bars, specifying the category positions and data values.
   - Optionally, set a custom color for the bars using `color="skyblue"`.
4. *Customization*:
   - Add labels for the X and Y axes using `plt.xlabel` and `plt.ylabel`.
   - Add a title for the plot using `plt.title`.
5. *Show the plot*: Use `plt.show()` to display the created bar plot.

Option 2: Stacked Bar Plot

LISTING 6.11: stacked_bar_chart1.py

```
import matplotlib.pyplot as plt

# Define data for each group (replace with your own)
categories = ["Category 1", "Category 2", "Category 3"]
data1 = [3, 5, 7]  # Group 1 values for each category
data2 = [2, 1, 4]  # Group 2 values for each category

# Create the stacked bar plot
plt.figure(figsize=(8, 6))  # adjust figure size if needed
bar_width = 0.35
index = range(len(categories))  # Positions for category bars

p1 = plt.bar(index, data1, bar_width, label="Group 1")
p2 = plt.bar([i + bar_width for i in index], data2, bar_
width, label="Group 2", bottom=data1)

# Customize the plot
plt.xlabel("Categories")
plt.ylabel("Value")
plt.title("Stacked Bar Plot")
plt.xticks([i + bar_width / 2 for i in index], categories)
# Set category labels
plt.legend()
plt.grid(axis="y")

# Show the plot
plt.tight_layout()
plt.show()
```

Explanation:

1. *Import libraries*: Same as Option 1.
2. *Define data*:
   - Define `categories` as in Option 1.
   - Define two lists, `data1` and `data2`, containing values for each category for two different groups.
3. *Bar plot creation*:
   - Use `plt.figure` to adjust the figure size if needed.
   - Define a `bar_width` for each bar.
   - Set `index` to represent the positions for category bars.
   - Use `plt.bar` twice to create separate bars for each group on top of each other:
   - `p1` for Group 1 values with position, width, label, and bottom set to 0.
   - `p2` for Group 2 values with position shifted by `bar_width`, width, label, and bottom set to the top of the Group 1 bars (`data1`).
4. *Customization*:
   - Same as Option 1, including labels, title, and X-axis ticks with adjusted positions.
   - Add a legend using `plt.legend()`.
   - Enable grid lines on the Y-axis for reference with `plt.grid(axis="y")`.
   - Use `plt.tight_layout()` to adjust spacing for stacked bars.
5. *Show the plot*: Same as Option 1.

Both options provide a starting point for creating bar plots in `Python`. Remember to adapt the data, bar styles, and customizations to match your specific requirements and desired visual representation of your data.

Figure 6.10 displays the bar chart that is rendered by launching the code in Listing 6.10.

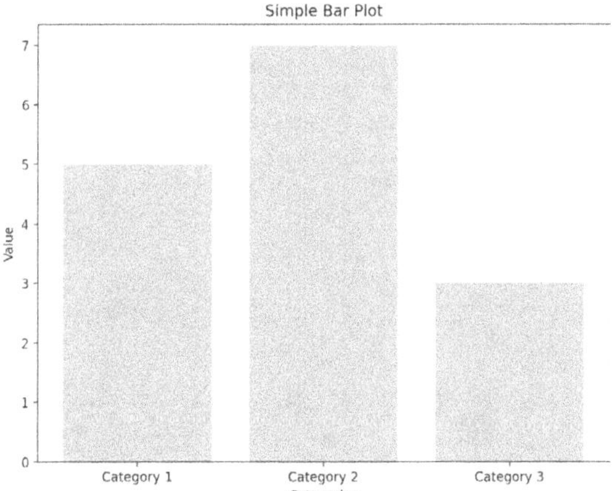

FIGURE 6.10. A bar chart with Matplotlib.

Here is an interesting detail: Bard "remembered" a previous request for generating a bar plot, and then provided a reminder, as shown here:

```
Bard: I apologize, I already provided Python code for a bar
plot earlier in our conversation. Did you have a specific
question about the previous code or a new aspect of a bar
plot you'd like me to address? Please clarify your request,
and I'll be happy to help further!
```

ME: please proceed and generate that Python code again

SCATTER PLOT WITH REGRESSION LINE

Display data points and a regression line to understand relationships. The following prompt was submitted to Bard in order to generate `Python` code for this section:

```
Please generate Python code for a scatter plot with a
regression line along with an explanation of the code.
```

Listing 6.12 displays the contents of `scatter_plot.py` that Bard generated in order to render a scatter chart using `Seaborn`.

_LISTING 6.12: scatter_plot.py_

```
import matplotlib.pyplot as plt
import numpy as np

# Define your data (replace with your own)
x = np.random.randn(100)  # Generate random X values
y = 2 * x + 3 + np.random.randn(100)  # Generate random Y
values with linear relationship

# Calculate regression line parameters
slope, intercept = np.polyfit(x, y, 1)  # Use polyfit for
linear regression

# Generate regression line points
x_line = np.linspace(min(x), max(x), 100)  # Create range
for line points
y_line = slope * x_line + intercept  # Calculate Y values
for line

# Create the plot
plt.figure(figsize=(8, 6))  # Customize figure size if needed
plt.scatter(x, y, s=20, c="blue", alpha=0.7, label="Data
Points")  # Plot data points with size, color, and label
plt.plot(x_line, y_line, color="red", linewidth=2,
label="Regression Line")  # Plot regression line with color
and linewidth
```

```
# Add labels and title
plt.xlabel("X-axis")
plt.ylabel("Y-axis")
plt.title("Scatter Plot with Regression Line")

# Show the plot
plt.legend()
plt.grid(True)  # Optional grid lines for reference
plt.show()
```

Explanation:

1. *Import libraries*: We import `matplotlib.pyplot` for plotting and `numpy` for calculations.
2. *Define data*: Replace `x` and `y` with your actual data lists or arrays.
3. *Regression line parameters*: Use `np.polyfit(x, y, 1)` to calculate the slope and intercept of the best-fit line for your data.
4. *Regression line points*: Generate a range of X values for the line and calculate the corresponding Y values using the slope and intercept.
5. *Plot creation*:
   - Use `plt.figure` to set the figure size.
   - Use `plt.scatter` to plot the data points with desired size, color, and alpha transparency.
   - Use `plt.plot` to plot the regression line with color and line width.
6. *Customization*:
   - Add labels for axes and title using `plt.xlabel`, `plt.ylabel`, and `plt.title`.
   - Display a legend with `plt.legend()`.
   - Optionally, enable grid lines with `plt.grid(True)`.
   - Customize colors, markers, line styles, and other visual elements as needed.
7. *Show the plot*: Use `plt.show()` to display the created scatter plot with the regression line.

This code provides a basic example of generating a scatter plot with a regression line. You can modify the data, calculations, and plot configurations to match your specific data and desired visual representation.

Scatter plots are great for visualizing relationships between two variables. `Seaborn` has a `regplot()` functions that not only plots the data points but also fits a regression line.

Figure 6.11 displays the scatter plot that is rendered by launching the code in Listing 6.12.

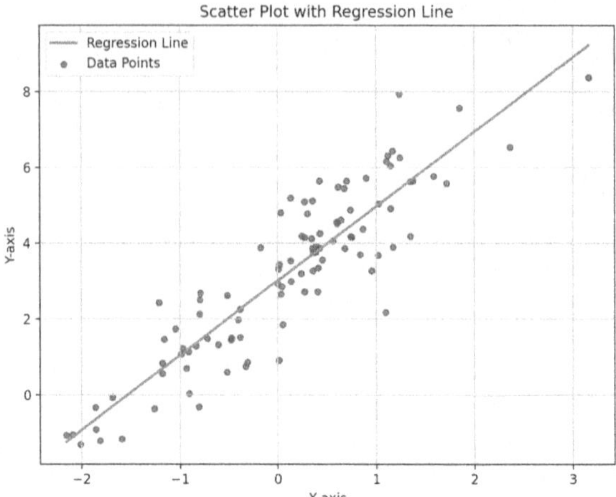

FIGURE 6.11. A scatter plot with Matplotlib.

HEATMAP FOR CORRELATION MATRIX WITH SEABORN

Heatmaps are powerful for representing matrices of data, with colors indicating magnitudes. A common use case is visualizing correlation matrices, which help in understanding relationships among different variables. Visualize correlations among multiple variables. The following prompt was submitted to Bard in order to generate `Python` code for this section:

```
Please generate Python code for a heatmap along with an
explanation of the code.
```

Bard generated the following text, asking for additional information:

```
Certainly! To provide the most relevant code, could you
tell me a bit more about the data you want to visualize
in the heatmap? Knowing the type of data (e.g., numerical
matrix, image, geographical), desired colormap, and any
specific customizations would help me generate the most
helpful code. The more details you share, the better I can
tailor the code to your needs.
```

Listing 6.13 displays the contents of `heatmap1.py` that Bard generated in order to render a line using `Matplotlib`.

LISTING 6.13: heatmap1.py

```
import numpy as np  # For numerical operations and array creation
import seaborn as sns  # For creating heatmaps
import matplotlib.pyplot as plt  # For displaying the heatmap
```

```
# 1. Create sample data (you'll replace this with your
actual data)
data = np.random.randint(low=1, high=100, size=(10, 10))  #
10x10 matrix of random numbers

# 2. Create the heatmap using Seaborn
sns.heatmap(data,  # Data to visualize
            cmap="coolwarm",  # Colormap (adjust as needed)
            annot=True,  # Annotate cells with values
            fmt=".1f",  # Format for annotations
            linewidths=0.5,  # Line width for cell borders
            cbar=True  # Show colorbar
           )

# 3. Customize and display the heatmap
plt.title("Sample Heatmap")  # Add a title
plt.show()  # Display the heatmap
```

Explanation:

```
    Import Libraries:
        numpy: Provides tools for numerical operations and
array manipulation.
        seaborn: Built on top of Matplotlib, offering high-
level functions for creating informative statistical
graphics, including heatmaps.
        matplotlib.pyplot: Provides the foundation for
plotting and visualization.

    Create Data:
        In this example, we create a 10x10 matrix of random
integers using np.random.randint. Replace this with your
actual data.

    Create Heatmap:
        sns.heatmap(data, ...): Generates the heatmap using
the provided data.
        Key arguments:
            cmap: Specifies the colormap to use. "coolwarm"
is a common choice for heatmaps, but you can explore other
options (e.g., "viridis", "plasma", "inferno").
            annot: If True, displays the actual data values
            within each cell.
            fmt: Formats the annotations if annot=True.
            linewidths: Adjusts the width of the lines
            separating cells.
            cbar: If True, includes a colorbar to interpret
            the color mapping.

    Customize and Display:
        plt.title(...): Adds a title to the plot.
        plt.show(): Renders the heatmap for viewing.
```

```
Remember:
    Replace the sample data with your actual data to
visualize your specific information.
    Explore different colormaps, annotations, and formatting
options to create heatmaps that effectively communicate your
insights.
```

Figure 6.12 displays the heatmap that is rendered by launching the code in Listing 6.13.

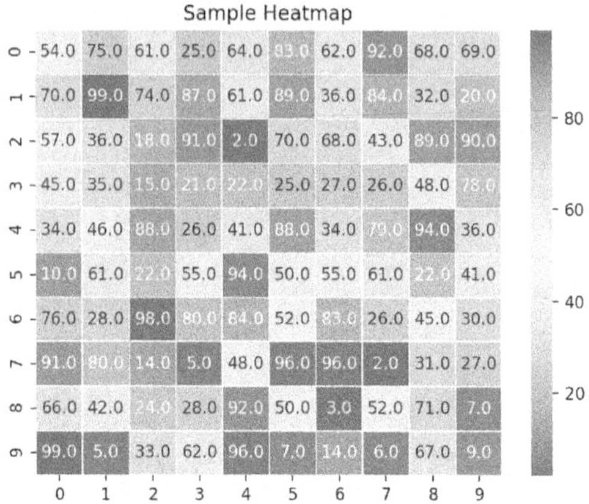

FIGURE 6.12. A heatmap with Matplotlib.

HISTOGRAMS WITH SEABORN

Histograms are powerful tools for visualizing the distribution of data. Seaborn's `histplot()` function provides a way to easily generate histograms with additional features like kernel density estimation. The following prompt was submitted to Bard in order to generate `Python` code for this section:

```
Please generate Python code for a histogram along with an
explanation of the code.
```

Listing 6.14 displays the contents of `histogram1.py` that Bard generated in order to render a histogram.

LISTI7NG 6.14: histogram1.py

```
import matplotlib.pyplot as plt
import seaborn as sns

def plot_histogram(data, column, bins=10):
    sns.histplot(data[column], bins=bins)
    plt.show()

# Usage
data = sns.load_dataset("iris")
plot_histogram(data, "sepal_length")
```

Listing 6.14 starts with two `import` statements and the `plot_histogram()` function that renders the histogram. The second half of Listing 6.14 initializes the `Pandas DataFrame data` with the contents of the `Seaborn` built-in dataset `iris`, and then invokes `plot_histogram()` with the variable `data`. Figure 6.13 displays the heatmap for the `Iris` dataset that is rendered by launching the code in Listing 6.14.

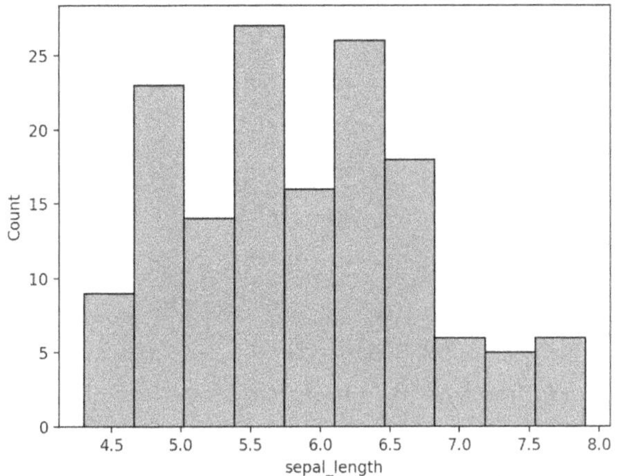

FIGURE 6.13. A Histogram with Matplotlib.

VIOLIN PLOTS WITH SEABORN

Violin plots offer a deeper understanding of the distribution of data. They combine the characteristics of box plots and histograms, showing the probability density of the data at different values. The following prompt was submitted to Bard in order to generate `Python` code for this section:

```
Please generate Python code for a violin plot along with an
explanation of the code.
```

Combine aspects of box plots and histograms to provide richer descriptions of data distributions. Listing 6.15 displays the contents of `violin_plots.py` that Bard generated in order to render a violin plot using Seaborn.

LISTING 6.15: violin_plots.py

```
import matplotlib.pyplot as plt
import seaborn as sns

# Define your data (replace with your own)
data = [
    # List of lists, each sublist representing data for a
group
    [3, 4, 5, 1, 2],
    [7, 8, 10, 9, 6],
```

```
    [12, 11, 13, 15, 14],
]

groups = ["Group 1", "Group 2", "Group 3"]  # Group labels
for each data list

# Create the violin plot
sns.violinplot(x=groups, y=data, showmedians=True,
inner="quart")  # Customize options

# Show the plot
plt.show()
TypeError: Neither the `x` nor `y` variable appears to be
numeric.
```

Explanation:

1. *Import libraries*: We import `matplotlib.pyplot` as `plt` for basic plotting and `seaborn` for enhanced violin plot functionalities.
2. *Define data*: Replace `data` with your actual data. Each sublist within the main list represents the data for a single group. Ensure all sublists have the same length.
3. *Group labels*: Define `groups` with labels corresponding to each data sublist in `data`.
4. *Violin plot creation*:
   - Use `sns.violinplot(x=groups, y=data)` to specify the X-axis positions (groups) and Y-axis data (sublists).
   - Optionally, set `showmedians=True` to display median lines within each violin.
   - You can modify the visualization using various keyword arguments like `inner="box"` to show boxplots within violins, `linewidth` for violin outlines, and `color` for group-specific colors.
5. *Show the plot*: Use `plt.show()` to display the created violin plot.

Further customization options:

- Adjust violin and box widths with `violin_scale` and `box_aspect`.
- Add quartiles and notches with `showmeans=True` and `draw_markers=True`.
- Modify the kernel density smoothing for violin shapes with `bw`.
- Add statistical comparisons between groups with `stat_func` and `linewidth`.
- Explore different colormaps and styles offered by `seaborn`.

Remember to adapt the data structure, group labels, and customization options to match your specific data and desired visual appearance of your violin plot.

ME: The Python code that you generated for a violin plot contains the following error:
TypeError: Neither the 'x' nor 'y' variable appears to be numeric. can you fix this error please?

Listing 6.16 displays the `Python` code that Bard corrected in order to display a violin plot.

Listing 6.16: violin_plots.py

```
import matplotlib.pyplot as plt
import seaborn as sns

# Define your data (replace with your own)
data = [
    # List of lists, each sublist representing data for a
group
    [3, 4, 5, 1, 2],
    [7, 8, 10, 9, 6],
    [12, 11, 13, 15, 14],
]

groups = ["Group 1", "Group 2", "Group 3"]  # Group labels
for each data list

# Transpose the data to have groups as columns
data = list(zip(*data))  # Transpose using zip

# Create the violin plot
sns.violinplot(data=data, showmedians=True, inner="quart")
# Customize options

# Set x-axis labels to group names
plt.xticks(ticks=range(len(groups)), labels=groups)

# Show the plot
plt.show()
```

Explanation of Changes:

Transpose Data: The error occurred because sns.violinplot() expects numeric data in columns, but your data was organized in rows. The zip(*data) function transposes the data, creating the expected format.

Remove Unnecessary x Argument: Since the data is now in the correct format, you don't need the x=groups argument in sns.violinplot(). The function automatically infers the x-axis labels from the column names.

Set X-Axis Labels: The plt.xticks() line ensures that the x-axis labels are set to your desired group names (groups).

With these adjustments, the code should now generate the violin plot correctly.

Figure 6.14 displays the violin plot that is rendered by launching the code in Listing 6.16.

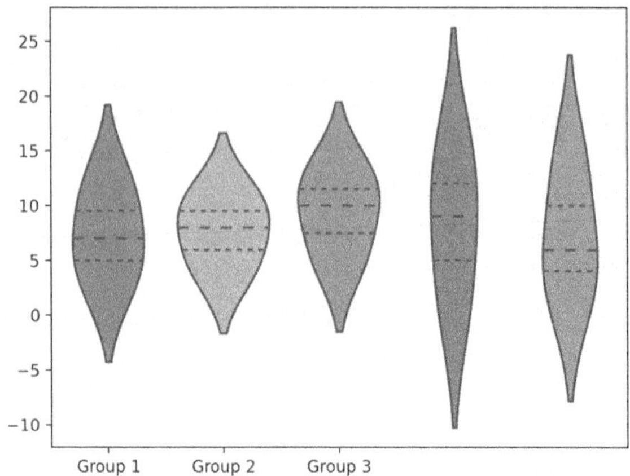

FIGURE 6.14. A Violin plot with Matplotlib.

SUMMARY

This chapter contains `Python`-based solutions generated by Bard to a variety of tasks. You learned about various types of charts and graphs, and when to use them, along with the advantages and disadvantages of each type of chart and graph.

You learned about data visualization using a popular open-source `Python`-based library called `Matplotlib` that can render numerous types of charts and graphs.

You also learned how to render bar charts, histograms, scatter plots, and violin plots. By mastering these techniques, one can craft compelling narratives from data, aiding in decision-making and insights generation. Keep in mind that a well-crafted visualization is worth a thousand rows of raw data.

INDEX

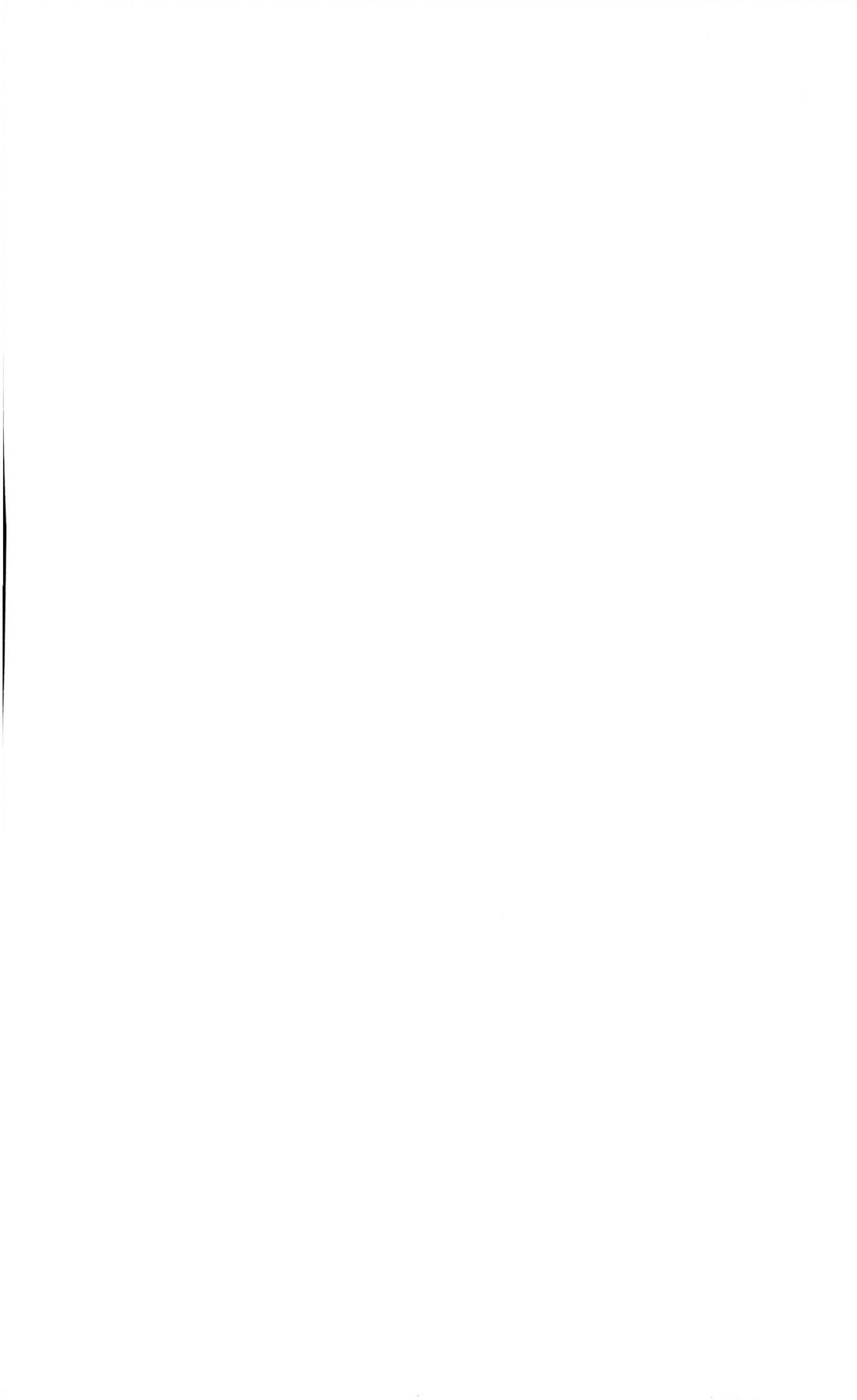

www.ingramcontent.com/pod-product-compliance
Lightning Source LLC
LaVergne TN
LVHW050635100826
845148LV00011B/1875

* 9 7 8 1 5 0 1 5 2 2 8 0 2 *